ENDORSEMENTS FOR
Glimpses: Two Stories of Hope and Healing

Jan de Chambrier's book, *Glimpses*, is both captivating and endearing. Jan's story resonates with the journal entries of her friend, Carrie Oliver, as she shares her personal journey with cancer. Her writing is honest, sincere, and inspiring. The character of a life fully devoted to God flows gently and tenderly from the pages of this book, engaging the reader with both spiritual truth and a heartfelt compassion for those who endure the rigors of surviving cancer. The story Jan presents is personal, but also profoundly reflective of the journey many cancer survivors experience. Her words offer a calm reassurance that cancer need not be the end of hope but can be the beginning of a new season of faith and a new opportunity to embrace all that is dear to us. The journey of two friends may end very differently, but they share the same destiny. At God's final Amen, we shall see the face of a loving God and our healing will indeed be complete. Jan's story will motivate readers to face life with determination and courage.

Rev. Cliff Ritter
Associate Pastor of Caring Ministries
The Woodlands United Methodist Church
The Woodlands, TX

This is an incredibly realistic book of faith and hope. The journey of these two women through cancer and with the Lord must be available to the millions of those in our country struggling with this disease.

Having lost my wife of forty-eight years to cancer, I can attest to the fact that this is an honest portrayal of this difficult journey. I knew Carrie all of her married life and performed the wedding ceremony for Gary and Carrie. I have seen and felt their pain and joys during their journey. I know their story will bless many lives.

Dr. H. Norman Wright
Marriage, Family and Child Therapist
Bakersfield, CA
Author of over 70 books, including *Surviving the Storms of Life*, *Reflections of a Grieving Spouse* and *Coping with Chronic Illness and Pain*

Glimpses is a book you'll find yourself reading more than once. I was so gripped by the stories of Jan and Carrie's twin journeys through cancer, each with a different ending (and beginning), that I raced through the first reading. The second time through it was with highlighter in hand, as the insights, illustrations and scriptural principles Jan relates are ones I want to share with others. This is a book I plan to purchase multiple copies of for those who are currently walking through "the valley of the shadow."

Maggie Wallem Rowe
Public Relations Specialist
Tyndale House Publishers
Wheaton, IL

Rarely does one come across a book that speaks with the truth and reality of life while unfolding a deep love relationship with the Lord. But this book DID IT! Never having any major health challenges, I felt through these two amazing women the compassion, understanding and connection with our Savior in their passion for healing and love of Him. This book shows that other things are truly unimportant.

Cynthia Kubetin Littlefield, MA, LPC
Director, Christian Counseling Center of Houston
Houston, TX
Author of *Shelter from the Storm* and *Beyond the Darkness*

As you read *Glimpses* you will come face-to-face with the teaching of two women: One through her final journey until she saw Jesus face-to-face, and one through her journey of illness and healing. There is a beauty in the intricacy of the 'tapestry' that God has woven through their stories. I know you will be struck through your reading more with Jesus than with either Jan or Carrie. This is a book worthy of adding to your library of spiritual formation.

Barb Roberts
Director of Caring Ministry
Cherry Creek Presbyterian Church
Englewood, CO
Author of *Helping Those Who Hurt: A Handbook for Caring and Crisis*

Glimpses

Glimpses

Two Stories
of Hope and
Healing

by

Jan de Chambrier & Carrie Oliver
Foreword and Afterword by Dr. Gary Oliver

Prayer Point Press

Glimpses
Two Stories of Hope and Healing
Jan de Chambrier and Carrie Oliver
Foreword and Afterword by Dr. Gary Oliver

© 2011 Jan de Chambrier
Published by Prayer Point Press
Cover design by Lynette Whitesell

Printed in the United States of America
August 2011

ISBN: 978-1-57892-064-8

For order information, visit www.jandechambrier.com. You can also find information about this book through Prayer Point Press at www.prayerpoint.com.

To Philippe de Chambrier,
my dearly beloved husband,
and the one who loves me as Christ loves the church.

Preface

There is no doubt in my mind that I was called to write this book with my dear friend, Carrie Oliver. Diagnosed with different kinds of cancer sixteen years apart, our meeting was God-designed and our relatively brief friendship a divinely pre-ordained sisterhood. God had impressed on both of us His desire that we share the testimonies of His faithfulness through our life experiences and particularly our journeys through cancer. Although Carrie had asked me to collaborate on this project with her in early April of 2007, we never got past the preliminary planning stages, as her health declined rapidly thereafter and she died on July 2 of that year. It was on the day of her memorial service that I sensed the Lord impress on me that this book would still be written, and by both of us. The means would be Carrie's online updates, which she called "A Journal of Hope." After receiving her husband Gary Oliver's permission and blessing to proceed with this in March of 2008, I fervently prayed for the Lord to show me a format and to divinely synthesize our two stories and writing styles in a way that would glorify Him and bring encouragement to others.

I have never experienced such a continual outpouring of God's Spirit as in the writing of this book. Perhaps because I knew that it was so far beyond my own ability, I trusted Him to do exceedingly abundantly more than I could ask or even imagine according to His power at work within me. I began by making a hard copy of Carrie's online journal updates, which totaled 126 pages. I then highlighted scripture references in yellow and passages that I could excerpt in pink, and categorized each entry by its predominant topic. I prayed each day for the Lord to guide me in the choice of the daily subject, and then chose a scripture on which to base the writing that day. I made the decision to graft our ideas together in the first person with direct quotations from Carrie's journal, and to separate our "voices" by spacing and font rather than quotation marks so as to make it appear more conversational: two friends comparing life experiences. I took the liberty of occasionally editing Carrie's entries, which I'm quite sure she would not have minded. I also received permission from Gary Oliver to use excerpts from his own updates on Carrie's website after her death.

A project of this magnitude is certainly the fruit of the labors of many, and I cannot adequately express my gratitude to Prayer Point Press editor Lynn Ponder. So evidently Spirit-filled and led, Lynn expertly and patiently guided me through choices I didn't even realize needed to be made, rather like a home builder leading a client through everything from plumbing fixtures to doorknobs to exterior finish, all the while shaping everything into a cohesive whole. If Lynn acted as the general contractor, cover artist Lynette Whitesell was the landscaper. Having not yet read the manuscript, Lynette responded to Lynn's synopsis of the book and managed to capture the heart and intent of Carrie's and my writing in an Ephesians 3:20—"exceedingly abundantly more than you can ask or even imagine"—style.

The title for this book is derived from the final chapter, "Glimpses." Carrie and I often talked about living every day as Jesus taught us to pray: "Your kingdom come, your will be done on earth as it is in heaven." We felt so privileged to see glimpses of His kingdom everywhere we looked! And now it is a privilege to share it with our brothers and sisters in Christ. Every chapter is intended only for the glory of God and for the edification of His people. May those who read it come to know more fully the love of Christ that surpasses all knowledge.

Contents

Foreword

This is a book about joy, victory, happiness and faithfulness. Yes, there's some sadness, sorrow, and goodbyes—but it is a book that has a happy ending! It's about the difference that friendship and faith can make in some of the darkest and most difficult realities of life. It's about hope. Not merely hope in spite of something, but a very real hope in the midst of something. This is a book on how to not just survive, but on how to thrive in the midst of difficulties, both big and small. When events in life work to rewrite your life story and you are overwhelmed with a tsunami of circumstances and a confusing range of emotions that you didn't want and don't understand, what do you do? How do you respond? Where can you go?

It was over twenty years ago that I was told that what doctors thought was just a benign growth in my mouth was actually cancer and that they were going to operate in two days. I stood there holding the phone and staring out the window. These things don't happen to me! These are the kinds of things I help others deal with. But me, have cancer? No way!

Six years ago, I sat in a doctor's office and heard him give that same diagnosis to my wife Carrie, except that hers was for metastatic pancreatic cancer with a prognosis of just three to six months. It was actually infinitely more painful for me to hear her diagnosis than it was to hear my own. Given the somber prognosis, little did I know that God in His goodness and grace had much

15

more than three months for Carrie to continue to be with us and impact her world.

Shortly after Carrie's diagnosis, I received a phone call from one of my Denver Seminary doctoral students, Stew Grant, at that time the Pastor of Caring Ministries at The Woodlands United Methodist Church. Stew told me that he had spoken with Jan de Chambrier, who with her husband Philippe was a vital part of their strategic prayer team, and that Jan would be willing to meet us at M.D. Anderson Cancer Center and pray with us.

I still remember Jan's first meeting with Carrie and how encouraged and overjoyed Carrie was to have a special God-given prayer warrior friend to come alongside her on her M.D. Anderson visits, especially those few checkups when I was unable to accompany her. I remember the joy of Jan, Philippe, Carrie and me laughing and praying together, especially as we discovered mutual friends and shared interests. I remember God manifesting His presence through the powerful and healing presence of friends.

As Jan shared the story of dealing with her own cancer and other challenges, including major losses in her life, it was clear that God had brought Jan and Carrie together for a special purpose: not just to comfort and encourage each other, but to be a beacon of encouragement to others. Both had experienced God's healing power in mighty ways, and shortly before her death, Carrie and I had several conversations about our sense that God might have them share their powerful stories through writing a book together.

As you read these true stories, you'll discover new ways to see the hand of our sovereign God in all that comes your way. It allows us to embrace, if not celebrate, the circumstances of our lives in ways that don't involve a pseudo-spiritual "denial" of the diagnosis and pain, but that allow us to put it into the bigger picture of what only He can see, a picture we can rely on and trust. A picture that, according to Romans 8:28, He can work together for good.

As I write this, I am recovering from my seventh cancer surgery and four months of a tough regimen of chemotherapy. However,

I have great joy—and my belief in the goodness, grace, mercy and lovingkindness of my Lord has never been greater. I daily experience sovereign joy. I have a hope not born out of denial, but cultivated from having walked through pain and the death of several loved ones, having experienced the sustained presence and power of God's promises in the midst of the darkness.

The real-life stories of Jan and Carrie, the very real valleys they have walked through, will inspire and encourage you and point you to a reservoir of resources that you can draw on and drink from, no matter how difficult the circumstances of your life.

Gary J. Oliver, Th.M., Ph.D.

The Lord will fight for you, and you shall hold your peace.
—Exodus 14:14 (NKJV)

1

Our Story

"I have an assignment for you, Jan, and her name is Carrie Oliver." I was talking one Sunday to the Pastor of Caring Ministries, Stew Grant, at our church. "I know her!" I exclaimed excitedly. "At least, I know all about her and have already been praying for her. She's a friend of my good friend Barb!" Stew elaborated, "Well, I want you to come alongside Carrie and be a friend to her when she comes to Houston for treatments at M.D. Anderson." "I can do that!" I affirmed, with the joy that comes only from knowing that the Lord is at work and about to do something amazing.

Carrie was diagnosed with metastatic cancer of the pancreas in May of 2005. Although we had both lived in Denver, Colorado for several years at the same time, we had never met and yet had a dear friend in common, Barb Tallant. When Carrie received her diagnosis, Barb called me and was deeply distressed. I began praying for Carrie because the Lord kept putting her on my heart and because I knew she was dear to Barb. I had also heard a Christian radio interview a few years earlier in which Carrie's husband Gary Oliver told of his own multiple battles with oral cancer. I remember being so impressed by his testimony. Even before we ever met, the Lord had laid the groundwork for a profound friendship with the Olivers.

The reason Stew had asked me to come alongside Carrie was that I am a cancer survivor and part of the intercessory prayer and healing ministry at The Woodlands United Methodist Church in The Woodlands, Texas, serving along with my husband Philippe and a dedicated team of prayer warriors. I was diagnosed with endometrial (uterine) cancer in April of 1990 during my first and only pregnancy. There followed many years of related health crises and a commensurate growth in my walk with the Lord as I learned firsthand of His faithfulness in every situation. I grew very committed to helping others walk this journey of faith, and also became a peer mentor at M.D. Anderson, sharing hope with those who have been recently diagnosed with similar cancers.

My first meeting with Carrie actually took place on Thursday, January 19, 2006. I had phoned her the evening before, knowing that she was by then in Houston for treatment, and was struck immediately by the warmth and sincerity—and yes, even joy in her voice as we chitchatted about the experiences we had in common and made plans for me to meet her at M.D. Anderson the next day. She told me that she would be having surgery to repair a stent and asked if I would come and pray with her.

I was quite frankly astonished the next afternoon when the nurse led me back to the pre-op area where Carrie was lying on a gurney being prepped for surgery. She didn't appear to me to be a "victim" of cancer; she was simply beautiful, with big aquamarine eyes, stylish blonde hair and a megawatt smile, alive in the joy of the Lord. As we embraced with hugs that held the promise of a heavenly sisterhood, my own walk through the valley of cancer flashed before me. How deceiving appearances can be!

Dr. Francis Major, the gynecologic oncologist who performed my surgery, had declared the day before my operation, "You appear to be so perfectly normal that if it hadn't been for your pregnancy, we would not have discovered this cancer for two more years." I would never have thought that cancer would happen to me; after all, I was strong, self-sufficient, exercised regularly, ate (mostly) right. Neither was Carrie a likely candidate for this dreaded disease. But the fact that we had both become involuntary members of a club no one ever wants to join formed part of the basis for our friendship. Infinitely overriding that designation, however, was our common membership in the body of Christ. This would be the bond that would forever unite our hearts in a unique testimony of God's abiding love and faithfulness in all circumstances.

CARRIE

Journal entry, January 22, 2006: A dear woman from (she names some mutual friends) church in The Woodlands joined me, Jan de Chambrier. Oh, what pure delight Jan is. Jan had cancer sixteen years ago and has been through it in terms of surgeries and fears and walking through her own cancer journey. I loved her from first sight. She sat with me and prayed with me.

Carrie's periodic visits to Houston were times I eagerly antici-pated, with so much to share about life and God's goodness and love. The frequency depended on whatever her current treatment protocol required, but would average about once a month. In be-tween, we exchanged frequent phone calls and e-mails, discussing anything and everything good friends share: her recipe for peaches and cream pie and my description of the beautiful fuchsia azaleas blooming in our neighborhood; new insights into old Oswald Chambers' entries or the plot of Lori Wick's latest novel; compari-sons of our sons and the challenges and victories of motherhood; our loving husbands and their sweet, funny ways; the students we mentored at JBU and Rice University. We would plan our meet-ings with the enthusiasm of a family reunion, yet it seemed almost incongruous that the venue was not the Galleria or the Museum of Fine Arts or the Cheesecake Factory, but the M.D. Anderson Cancer Center. Whether it was sharing a sandwich in the lovely atrium café, browsing in the gift shop, getting our daily workout treading the sky bridge to the parking garage, or reciting favorite scripture passages as we waited for appointments, memories were being made with each encounter and the bonds of our sisterhood became so strong that Carrie eventually started calling me "Twin"!

CARRIE

E-mail, April 3, 2007: Had a thought today! I think it would be a blessing to write a book together on walking through cancer. Let's do that someday.

Well, I must confess that this particular thought had occurred to me many times, but I was reluctant to broach it with Carrie because she was already a several-times published author and I thought it would be presumptuous of me, a complete rookie, to even suggest it. However, I seized the moment and responded immediately that I would love to do this together, and we soon made plans for me to go to Siloam Springs for a writing retreat together to outline the book. Tragically, the Oliver's middle son, Matt, died unexpectedly a few weeks later, and Carrie's health declined rapidly. She joined Matt in heaven on July 2, 2007.

On the day of Carrie's memorial service, I sat in that bizarre state of abject grief overlaid with utter faith knowledge that she was home in heaven with our Savior. I listened to one testimony after another of how she had touched lives for Christ: her family, friends, colleagues, clients. Then I sensed the Lord impressing on me, "This book will still be written." I really had to ask Him about that one! "How, Lord? She's no longer here." He then reminded me of Carrie's website and online journal, "A Journal of Hope" (www.carries health.com). The site was suggested and designed by Carrie's friend Catherine Arnsperger, who thought that Carrie could share on the Web her progress, her heart, and what God was teaching her. Carrie had started it on June 14, 2005, shortly after her diagnosis.

Suddenly I saw light! When I asked her husband Gary about using Carrie's reflections from her journal as her voice in this book, he promised me that he would pray about it and let me know. In late March, 2008, I was thrilled when Gary met Philippe and me for dinner and gave me his blessing to proceed with this project. Later on, when I asked him why he had agreed to allow me to write this book and even to collaborate with me on it, Gary wrote: "While I wanted to think and pray about it, my immediate gut response was a strong 'yes.' God had brought you two together for a variety of reasons, and I didn't believe that her death was the end of what God wanted to do. Perhaps Carrie's death was a different kind of beginning than any of us had anticipated."

Our intent is for all cancer patients and their families and caregivers who read this to have the assurance that God is their ever-present help in trouble and will never leave or forsake them… that He turns to good those things that were intended for evil… that He works all things together for good for those who love Him and are called according to His purpose…that His mercies are new every morning, and His faithfulness is great. Praise be to the God and Father of our Lord Jesus Christ, the Father of compassion and the God of all comfort, who comforts us in all our troubles, so that we can comfort those in any trouble with the comfort we ourselves have received from God (II Corinthians 1:3-4). May He alone be glorified!

> **Gracious Lord,** I offer to you this story of your faithfulness to me and to my friend, Carrie Oliver. I thank you that you have loved us with your everlasting love and surrounded us with your everlasting arms. I thank you that both of us have been healed: mine on this earth, and Carrie's complete healing in Heaven. May the words that follow be acceptable in your sight and healing to your precious children who are suffering. I ask this in the name of Jesus, our Savior and Lord, Amen.

I remain confident of this: I will see the goodness of the Lord in the land of the living. Wait for the Lord; be strong and take heart and wait for the Lord. —Psalm 27:13-14

2

Diagnosis Cancer

The hemorrhage began on Good Friday, April 6, 1990. My doctor, Leonard Cedars, told me that I had just miscarried but that it was likely that I had been carrying twins and that the other fetus was still viable. Holding forth hope, Philippe and I prayed fervently and went faithfully every other day to have my hormone levels checked. Our spirits rose proportionately with those levels, and my dear husband, a captain for Continental Airlines, took time off from flying to be at my side continually. He even endured seemingly endless run-throughs of the opera *Faust* as he accompanied me to Opera Colorado rehearsals. Finally, Dr. Cedars felt that we had passed the point of danger, and Philippe left on a trip. No sooner had he lowered the garage door than I was overcome by a crushing pain in my abdomen. I was rushed to the hospital where it was determined that I had an ectopic (tubular) pregnancy. Emergency surgery was performed at Swedish Medical Center in Denver, and when I awakened from the anesthesia, Dr. Cedars explained that he had been able to save my fallopian tubes and that hopefully we would be able to conceive again in the future. Nevertheless, Philippe and I grieved the loss of the two children we would not raise, but instead would meet one day in heaven.

On my second post-operative visit, I was expecting to be led to one of the familiar examining rooms when the nurse very gently said, "Dr. Cedars would like to see you in his office." I felt my blood run cold and my stomach plummet like a sixty-story express elevator, and had the absurd thought that this must be what unruly kids feel like when they're called to the principal's office. It just couldn't be good news. My doctor, with the greatest tact and compassion, told me that he had experienced a shadow of a doubt about the pathology report following my surgery, and unknown to me, had sent slides to three leading pathologists around the country. His task that day was to tell me that they had come back revealing adenocarcinoma of the uterus. As I sat there in surreal disbelief, the only thing I could think to say was, "It must be really hard to be a doctor." Dr. Cedars then outlined a tentative plan for my treatment, which would include the removal of my entire reproductive system as soon as possible, and said that he would call my husband that evening. I walked out of the office numb and feeling so very much alone.

I am certain that the angels of the Lord led me home as I drove that day, since I was crying so profusely that I could hardly see the road. When I arrived home, knowing that Philippe was on a trip and still probably in the air, I phoned my dear friend Irene, who assured me that she would be over right away. I then called my parents, and my dad answered the phone, having stayed home from the office with a cold. I could hardly speak, but sobbed out, "The doctor says I have cancer!" There was a shocked silence, and then the pastor in my dad (who was an ordained Presbyterian minister) took over. He instructed me to call our church and ask them to begin praying for me, to which I responded, "But Dad, then everyone will know!" And he wisely countered, "You need their prayers more than you need your privacy." That was a life lesson for me. In obedience, I called our church and support began pouring in immediately. Barb Roberts, the director of Caring Ministry at our church, offered to pick up Philippe at the airport. In the meantime, he had phoned and I blurted out the incomprehensible news to him.

The presence of the Lord came over him in an utterly profound way and he spoke words of comfort to me with an assurance and authority that could only be from God.

With each day as we began gathering information to determine the treatment protocol, the common theme was that the Lord was always at our side, and on our side. The intimacy with which He orchestrated details was undeniable. After conferring with two experts on this type of cancer, it was becoming clear that the removal of all of my reproductive organs was clearly the accepted treatment, possibly followed by a six-week course of radiation. Not having borne a child yet, we were heartsick over this news. I learned through Dr. Cedars of a physician at M.D. Anderson, Dr. Creighton Edwards, who was conducting experimental trials in which eggs were extracted following high dosages of hormones so that there could potentially be a surrogate pregnancy. We clung to this hope, but after several days, had not heard back from the doctor. We felt led to go to the mountains for a time of retreat to pray about out decisions, and then had to unexpectedly return for a forgotten item. During that small window of opportunity, Dr. Edwards called from Houston, and after painstakingly listening to my story and weighing the pros and cons, he determined that this approach would not be viable for me. We gave thanks to God for this clarity and provision, even as we released our hope to Him.

My final dilemma in proceeding with such radical surgery was this: what if, by His hand, the Lord had already healed me, and the surgeons were to go in and find no cancer in the organs they had just removed? I asked God to provide someone with great discernment to help me with this. We were led through the counsel of LeAnne Payne, founder of Pastoral Care Ministries, to call Dr. Diane Komp at Yale University, who in turn referred us to a woman of deep Christian faith named Ginny whom we did not know, but who was very gifted in spiritual discernment. I would never have anticipated her words: "Jan, have the surgery. If I had done what the doctors told me to do, I would not be dying of cancer right now." Now that was a definitive answer. It became so clear that the common thread in this entire experience was the extent to which God was going to reveal His hand and His sovereign will over every circumstance. That intricacy of detail brought us so much peace, knowing that He was in control even when we felt so very out of control.

CARRIE

Journal entry, May 17, 2005: During the first few days after my diagnosis, so similar to many of you going through crisis, I felt an onslaught of emotions, most of which could come under the good ol' category of fear. I mean, what else does someone feel when, after a CT scan, the technician says that the doctor will be calling you as soon as possible? The doctor did exactly that and "invited" us to come to the office to talk with him. We all know what that means. We arrived at the office and listened with those ringing ears one gets when the news is difficult. That, in fact, I had a very large tumor in my pancreas and that he would like to send me to Kansas City to see a surgeon there to remove it.

We received a call that afternoon from Dr. Delcore in Kansas City and drove up the next afternoon with my x-rays to see him. Gary and I sat in his office (for an eternity) as he reviewed the scan, and watched him as he walked into the room, knowing the look on his face was less than hopeful. Don't you love those words, "Has anyone prepared you for how serious this tumor is?"

Once again, the ringing ears and need to disassociate, but I looked into his face and worked hard to hear every word he had to say, meanwhile melting into my husband's arms. My tumor was large and wrapped around a major blood vessel. Can't operate on that kind or I would bleed to death. We talked for at least an hour. I needed a stent to relieve the pressure on my bile duct, so he set that right up with a physician the next afternoon. I needed official biopsies of the type of cancer that would be done at the same time. I also saw the head of oncology that afternoon. Everyone is so thorough at KU Med!

Sometimes you need the illusion that if they miss it, then it isn't there. They found a lymph node in my neck nobody else had seen and ordered a chest CT to be done the next week and a biopsy of the node. My lungs were clear, but that node had adenocarcinoma, the same cancer as in the pancreas. At this time, we talked about going to M.D. Anderson. Our appointment was set for

Tuesday, May 31 with the head of gastroenterology, a dear, knowledgeable, positive and very hopeful physician, Dr. Abbruzzese. We didn't talk staging or prognosis (yes, I am beyond one and two, and yes, I have metastasis), but what is important is that there is hope for a battle!

Two very different types of cancer; two very similar reactions: the sense of unreality pervading every moment, so surreal that it is forever embedded in the fiber of your being; and, like soldiers in any battle, the beginning of a bond that glues kindred hearts together in a way that few other things can. The beginning of the realization that life on earth is truly temporary and is our opportunity to become intimately acquainted with our Maker, to share His love with those whom He has placed in our lives, and to bring glory to Him in all circumstances. Carrie and I simply delighted in sharing with each other, as well as with anyone who would listen, the stories of God's faithfulness in every situation. One of the greatest things anyone has ever said to me was something she shared more than once: "Jan, if it took getting cancer to get to know you, then it was worth it." And I can say the same, dear Carrie.

Father God, we have seen over and over that you do work all things together for good for those who love you and are called according to your purpose. You tell us that these "light and momentary troubles" are achieving for us an eternal glory that far outweighs them all! We have seen the evidence of your goodness in the land of the living. Lord, help us to live each day with the knowledge that it is a gift from you to bring you glory. Thank you that nothing, not even cancer—especially not cancer—can separate us from your love that is in Christ Jesus! To you alone be the glory, now and forever. Amen.

You are holy, O You who inhabit the praises of Israel.
—Psalm 22:3 (NASB)

3

Praise

My dear husband Philippe had just disembarked from his flight when he phoned from Denver International Airport to tell me that he was back from his trip. "The doctor says I have cancer!" I blurted out with sobs. For a moment, there was stunned silence; then words of reassurance as he told me that he would soon be home. As soon as he hung up, the Holy Spirit whispered to him, "Praise me." Philippe thought this was absolutely not something worthy of praise. However, he heard again, "Praise me now." Wanting to be obedient, but feeling ridiculous walking through the airport in his captain's uniform with tears streaming down his face, he said, "Well, Lord, can I maybe just…hum?" He began to softly intone every hymn and praise song that came to mind, and before long, he was actually singing. By the time he arrived at our home, he had the joy of the Lord as his strength and was able to assure me of God's sovereign plan for this uncharted journey we were embarking on together.

As I reread Carrie's journal, I was struck by the awareness that she began incorporating a praise section at the end of each journal entry shortly after her diagnosis: "Praise that I know God is at work!" "Praise for the worship music that is now on my mini iPod!" "Praise for my God in heaven who loves me and is still bending down to hear me;" "Praise for God's truth in His Word!" "Praise for the love of friends that keeps me going;" "Praise for my church and the body of Christ that loves me well" ... ad infinitum. With each entry, the presence of the Lord seems to be more apparent as He inhabits those praises. The dark and ominous cloud of cancer begins to yield to the light and hope that is Christ.

I love to go to the Psalms to praise God, and being a musician, I appreciate that there are so many that are already set to music that I can use to worship the Lord in singing. Psalm 8 declares, "O Lord, our Lord, how majestic is your name in all the earth! You have set your glory above the heavens. From the lips of children and infants you have ordained praise because of your enemies, to silence the foe and the avenger." Just this morning, I was marching with our two energetic Italian greyhounds around a little pond near our home, singing at the top of my lungs, "The Lord is my light and my salvation—whom then shall I fear? The Lord is the strength of my life—of whom shall I be afraid?" from Psalm 27. Singing praises to God calls my heart to worship like nothing else!

Sometimes praising God simply feels like a sacrifice, as it was for my husband when he learned of my cancer diagnosis, but the psalmists weren't exempt from that, either. Psalm 77 is one that begins as a lament and ends in praise:

> I cried out to God for help; I cried out to God to hear me. When I was in distress, I sought the Lord; at night I stretched out untiring hands and my soul refused to be comforted. I remembered you, O God, and I groaned; I mused, and my spirit grew faint. You kept my eyes from closing; I was too troubled to speak. I thought about the former days, the years of long ago; I remembered my songs in the night. My heart mused and my spirit inquired: "Will the Lord reject us forever? Will He never show His favor again? Has

His unfailing love vanished forever? Has His promise failed for all time? Has God forgotten to be merciful? Has He in anger withheld His compassion?" Then I thought, "To this I will appeal: the years of the right hand of the Most High." I will remember the deeds of the Lord; yes, I will remember your miracles of long ago. I will meditate on all your works and consider all your mighty deeds. Your ways, O God, are holy; what God is so great as our God? You are the God who performs miracles; you display your power among the peoples. With your mighty arm you redeemed your people, the descendants of Jacob and Joseph.

To praise God is an act of obedience. We don't have to feel like it; we must simply act on it. The Holy Spirit does the rest. I remember sitting in yet another windowless, impersonal examining room at M.D. Anderson with Carrie and Gary as we anxiously awaited the news that her physician, Dr. James Abbruzzese, would bring with her latest test results. As I had asked the Lord how we might use the time together that morning, I was led to tuck some copies of Sylvia Gunter's *Prayer Portions* into my ever-expanding bag, and gave the Olivers each a copy. With that mutual economy of explanation that seems to be factored into fellowship with other believers, we simply began to recite from our hearts the attributes of God: "My comforter…my deliverer…my daily manna…my encourager…my hope of glory living in me…" and it was indeed glorious. I wondered afterwards if that room glowed with the glory of the Lord! By the time Dr. Abbruzzese arrived, the peace of God that surpasses all understanding was guarding our hearts and minds in Christ Jesus.

Praising God has increasingly become a joyful part of my life because I have seen without exception that He keeps His promise to inhabit the praises of His people. However, it is not always my first inclination, especially when I am suffering.

In April 2008, I was nearly unable to walk due to two herniated disks in my lower spine. Writhing in agony one sleepless night, I finally decided to put into practice what I knew to be true. As my husband came alongside me, we began to declare the names of God and His faithfulness to us. At first, I felt almost hypocritical because it was not consistent with what I was feeling: utterly exhausted, gripped with pain no matter what my posture, and wondering if God was really listening. However, as I began to recount His faithfulness to me and to praise Him for who He is, the presence and majesty of God overwhelmed me to such an extent that the pain became far less significant than the glory of the Lord. I finally understood why God places such an emphasis on praising Him: when He is at the epicenter of our beings, we cannot be overtaken by pain and fear. He is inhabiting our praises! He who is in us is greater than he who is in the world! Nothing can separate us from His love!

I spoke to a young women's group at our church recently on praising God, and as I prepared for the talk, I developed an acrostic on the word HOSANNA (which means "Save us!") to help them remember some steps to praise:

H Hear God's voice: "Be still, and know that I am God." Know that Jesus is standing at the door and knocking, waiting for you to open the door. Greet Him with praise!

O Obey God's voice and offer a sacrifice of praise, knowing that He will inhabit that praise!

S Sing and shout to the Lord! Express the emotions you are feeling and release them to your Creator and Sustainer.

A Affirm His promises, such as Philippians 4:4-7, "Rejoice in the Lord always, and again I will say it: Rejoice! Let your gentleness be evident to all. The Lord is near. Do not be anxious about anything, but in everything, by prayer and petition with thanksgiving, present your requests to God. And the peace of God, which surpasses all understanding, will guard your hearts and minds in Christ Jesus."

N (K)neel before Him! There are postures of prayer that reflect our present emotions as well as convey praise, adoration, supplication, surrender, submission, and so much more. Allow the Lord to fill your physical body with manifestations of praise to Him. Raise your arms to the heavens! Clap your hands! Dance! Lie facedown before our Almighty Maker in total surrender.

N Name His names! There are many names for God in scripture, including the Hebrew names that convey different aspects of His character: Jehovah (I Am); Jehovah Rohi (my Shepherd); Jehovah Tsidkenu (my Righteousness); Jehovah Rapha (my Healer); Jehovah Nissi (my Banner); Jehovah Shalom (my Peace); Jehovah Jireh (my Provider). Sometimes when I am struggling a bit and feeling resistance to praising God, I will play my version of the Alphabet Game. I start with the letter "A" and say a word that describes God, like "Alpha" or "Almighty." I then proceed through the entire alphabet, making little allowances for pesky letters like X and Z (although sometimes I'll indulge myself with "eXcellent" and Zealous. Hey, they work for me!) By the time I've gone through the alphabet, the Lord is inhabiting my praises!

A Adore Him! Adoration is the result, or culmination, of our praise. Through willfully and obediently choosing to praise God, we then come to a place of adoration. He truly becomes our All in all, the Fairest of 10,000, the Name above every other name, the Desire of our hearts, the Light of the world. "Praise the Lord, O my soul; all my inmost being, praise His holy name. Praise the Lord, O my soul, and forget not all His benefits.

He forgives all my sins and heals all my diseases; He redeems my life from the pit and crowns me with love and compassion. He satisfies my desires with good things, so that my youth is renewed like the eagles. Praise the Lord, you His angels, you mighty ones who do His bidding, who obey His word. Praise the Lord, all His heavenly hosts, you His servants who do His will. Praise the Lord, all His works everywhere in His dominion. Praise the Lord, O my soul" (Psalm 103:1-5; 20-22).

Almighty God, we do praise your Name, for you alone are worthy of praise. Now to you who alone are able to sustain us and present us blameless before your glorious throne with great joy, we offer you all glory, honor, majesty and praise, knowing that you hear and inhabit what we proclaim in your Name. Amen.

For God has not given us a spirit of fear, but of power and of love and of a sound mind. —2 Timothy 1:7 (NKJV)

4
Fear

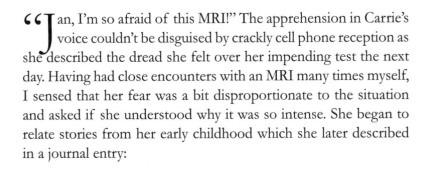

"Jan, I'm so afraid of this MRI!" The apprehension in Carrie's voice couldn't be disguised by crackly cell phone reception as she described the dread she felt over her impending test the next day. Having had close encounters with an MRI many times myself, I sensed that her fear was a bit disproportionate to the situation and asked if she understood why it was so intense. She began to relate stories from her early childhood which she later described in a journal entry:

CARRIE

Journal entry, April 4, 2006: As a child, I had several experiences where I was in places that felt like risks to me. I got into my aunt's drugs at the age of three and had my stomach pumped; had my tonsils out at four and remember the doctor telling the nurses to hold my hands and feet down as he came at me with the ether pad (he had not had "Talking to Small Children before Surgery 101"). I got caught in an elevator by myself at age three. At age ten, several of us were in a raft jumping off into the lake. I jumped off and came up under the boat. They kept moving the boat to find me, so I could not get out from under the boat, but finally did. These are my childhood experiences that have set me up for claustrophobia.

Despite Carrie's powerful faith in God and her training and experience as a skilled clinical therapist, there was a visceral root of fear that caused her to dread being in what she felt was a similar situation. By bringing her fear into the open and allowing the light of Christ to shine on it, she began to see that Jesus had been with her all along; He had never left her or forsaken her, and He would be with her in that MRI machine the next day.

I began to examine my own fear responses that belie what I know to be true. I saw myself as a tear-stained little girl of five, standing with one foot on the first step of a train in Chicago's cavernous Union Station, carrying a cold, half-eaten hamburger wrapped in a paper napkin. My parents had to send my seven-year-old brother Tim and me to our aunt and uncle in Springfield, IL due to my mother's lengthy hospitalization. I never realized the impact that situation had on me until Tim asked me a couple of years ago, "Were you as terrified on that train as I was?" YES! Big time YES! I now understand that the reason I have such difficulty going to any new place alone has its roots in this memory. I can be in my own little white Nissan Versa with a full tank of gas, a GPS, a printout of MapQuest, a twelve-pack of Evian, and a bag of Dove chocolates to console me, and I will still have heart palpitations! But by speaking the fear into the open, remembering that Jesus was there with me when the first fear gripped me, and has always brought me through no matter how many times it has happened since then, I can begin to experience healing. Hebrews 13:8 reassures us, "Jesus Christ is the same yesterday and today and forever."

Carrie overcame her fear of claustrophobia that day in the MRI because she faced it with Jesus holding her through it.

CARRIE

E-mail to friends and family: My I.V. was put in and off I went with Ehab [Dr. Ehab Hanna and his wife Sylvie are very close friends of the Olivers who opened their home and hearts countless times to Carrie and Gary when they came to Houston for treatments] who would be with me along with my good-natured male tech, Whitney. Together we were a team! I got on the table and earplugs were inserted into my ears as the test is extremely loud and noisy. Into the tube I went. At this time I was tired from the day and felt that it was now time to trust the Lord; He had me there and He would hold me through it. The noise began. I found the noise to be rhythmic and it helped me to keep my thoughts on task. I prayed a lot over my prayer list I had made that day. I quoted the scriptures God gave me in the last two weeks and as always, Exodus 14:14 was a base verse for me. "I will fight the battle for you; all you have to do is be still!" And still I was! I sang worship songs in my head. When the test was done, I asked if I had won any awards for lying perfectly still for one and a half hours. My reward was getting to go back to the Hanna's house. I do thank the Lord for His very present help in time of need and while this would be no big deal for many people, it was for me and an experience that required falling, once again, into the arms of Jesus and laying there allowing Him to comfort me. Thank you to those of you that prayed for me. I did not have one panic moment upon being in that tube.

The first year following my diagnosis with endometrial cancer was the most fearful year of my life. Despite early detection, surgery to remove all of my reproductive organs, and a clean pathology report afterwards, my mind would not lay this to rest. No amount of reassurance on the part of my long-suffering husband, endless conversations with my mom telling me that many, many people survive cancer, medical statistics favoring the likelihood that I would beat this illness, or repeated visits to my medical team could convince me that I was going to live. To a great degree, fear became the cancer. It was doing far more damage in my life than the actual physical disease had accomplished. The manifestation of my fear was like the medical equivalent of Baskin-Robbins' 31 Flavors! What symptom would be featured today? (Rocky Road, no doubt!) Who should I go to see, and what tests should I have?

During that year, I was in a doctor's office at least once a month, and had every diagnostic test known to man- and womankind: pelvic biopsy, MRI of the brain, cystoscopy of the bladder—you name it.

I would no sooner return from yet another procedure than I would plug in a new symptom to take its place; it was a veritable non-stop relay race. Finally, my dear Philippe was prompted to "speak the truth in love," a verse from Ephesians 4:15 that has since become a favorite of mine. He gently said, "Jan, don't you think that the same God who allowed you against all odds to become pregnant, and then revealed this otherwise-undetectable cancer by sacrificing the lives of our twins, has a plan for your life?" I don't recall any one statement ever having quite the immediate impact that one had on me. It was as if the scales fell off my eyes and I was unshackled from the bondage that had held me captive for so long. What was it? It was the TRUTH! Jesus says in John 8:32, "You will know the truth, and the truth will set you free."

Carrie's experience with cancer was perhaps more ominous than mine because of the nature of her disease and its prognosis. However, fear is fear, and must be brought before the only One who can conquer it: the Lord Jesus Christ.

CARRIE

Journal entry, August 7, 2005: When I let me eyes turn right or left, (I) can allow fear to creep in. The what-ifs start screaming at me. It is at that moment I straighten out my eyes on my path I am following and recount the verses such as Mark 11:22-25 and James 5. When I cry out to the Lord, He reminds me that I must not doubt His love and care and involvement in my life, and He is healing me. Healing my sin, my fear, my doubts, my selfishness, my pride—and He is at work in my physical body as well.

Journal entry, August 16, 2006: The hard thing about fear is that no person can make it better for you. Only you can get it under control and that means a lot of going to the Word and truth of God and going to God Himself. I have been talking to Him a great deal. The very wonderful news is that He is faithful and this morning I was feeling much less fearful. The scriptures that I go to often are "Trust in the Lord with all your heart and lean not unto your own understanding" (Proverbs 3:5); "Do not be anxious about anything..."

(Philippians 4:6); "Do not be afraid of the dangers by day or the terrors at night" (Psalm 91); and so many more. The Word is my friend when the strength of others cannot supply. I am constantly in this learning process and know that peace on earth is one hard thing to accomplish, but is oh, so sweet when experienced.

Precious Lord, We know that the only true antidote to fear is Jesus, who canceled its power when He gave His life on the cross. Thank you for giving us a Redeemer who knows our every need and who feels the depth of our pain and fear. We are so relieved that we can bring all of these needs before you without feeling inadequate or being judged; you tell us to cast our cares on you, because you care for us. Help us to fix our eyes on Jesus, the Author and Perfector of our faith, knowing that His love is perfect, and perfect love casts out fear. In Jesus' name, Amen.

Let us hold unswervingly to the hope we profess, for he who promised is faithful. —Hebrews 10:23

5

Hope

C ARRIE
Journal entry, June 20, 2005: Recently we received an article written by a friend of ours, Dr. Archibald Hart. He writes so eloquently on the experience of hope, what happens when we have it, and when we lose it.

> *You must never give up hope. No matter how bad the situation is or how despairing your circumstances are, you must never, NEVER give up hope. Never, never, never. Never give up hope for an ailing partner. Never give up hope for your children. Never give up hope for yourself. Why? Because if you give up on hope, you give up on life itself. If hope dies, you die. As a friend of mine once said, "As long as you keep hope alive, hope will keep you alive."*

Why hope when circumstances are hopeless? Because we were created for hope. Our bones were bred for hope. Our lungs can't breathe, our hearts won't beat and our spirits can't thrive without it. God placed us in a world over which we have little control. And, as if to compensate for this helplessness, He placed in our souls the capacity to hope—to hope for better times, to dream of better places, to pray for better outcomes, to seek better ways through life. Hope is more than optimism. Optimism is what we generate. Hope is God-given: a

powerful, spiritual and psychological means for transcending the circumstances.
Hebrews 6:19 tells us that Christian hope is a "sure and steadfast anchor for
the soul." But this hoping comes only as a gift of grace and is powerfully linked
to the promises of God. In fact, they are inseparable. Because you believe God's
promises, you can hope in the future. Without the future, there is nothing to
hope in. There is only fear, and fear leads us to a very dark place.

Dealing with cancer is definitely a powerful instigator for contemplating hope. My friend PJ, who has endured brain cancer for six years, shared her thoughts on hope in an e-mail I received just this morning:

> I believe that we experience hope on several different emotional levels. I think one could be called "casual hope." This would be where you hope to catch the green light; you hope there isn't a long line at the bank; you hope you are not late to the meeting; you hope it doesn't rain. It is a hope that exists in all of us, yet we rarely would consider this as being hope. Yet it is. I can picture a small child walking with his father. The child's tiny hand and little fingers are wrapped around the pinkie finger of the dad. The little child has hope, not even knowing really what hope is yet. The hope would be that his father is loving and protecting him. Like a father here on earth loves and takes care of his children, we have a heavenly Father who loves and desires nothing more than to take care of His children. I picture in my mind Jesus extending His open hand from the glory of heaven down to me. I hold my hand up to His and wrap my fingers around His little finger. He allows me to choose how I want to hold onto Him, with the expectation of fulfillment.
>
> The second level of hope I like to call "sincere hope." This to me is when someone says, "I hope you feel better" when you are sick, or "I hope to see you again

real soon!" There are those who speak hope for world peace. When these words are spoken to another, they are usually with the utmost, heartfelt sincerity. This level begins to define more clearly what hope is to me. I picture a world without war, without poverty and hunger, without any hate—and with the expectation of fulfillment.

The third level of hope becomes very difficult for me to describe. This feeling of hope is for anyone who has ever been diagnosed with a life-threatening disease; for those that have sat beside the bed of a dying loved one or friend; for those with an unbearable crisis in their life. Our hearts get broken and weigh heavily upon us. It is in these situations that one can hardly speak. So, I will call this one "whispering hope." This is when we fall on our knees and whisper prayers to God. We pray for healing, for strength, comfort, peace—for a miracle. I picture again my fingers wrapped around Jesus' little finger. I can see it is no longer enough for me; I now see Jesus stretching His hand out as wide as possible, making a way for me to climb into His hand so that He may now carry me through my difficult times. This is what hope means to me.

Carrie reiterates the message of hope some six months later in her entry.

CARRIE

Journal entry, January 6, 2006: I have absolutely no worldly control—none! I do have heavenly hope and that is much more powerful than any worldly power or control. As I look at the New Year, "hope" is still my truth and gift of mercy from the Lord that I hold very tightly to. Hope comes from faith and strong faith always brings great glory to God. Each day this defines my meaning and I pray that in this fresh new year of 2006, even more faith and hope will bring my Holy Father great glory. I hope that my actions, my words,

*my secret thoughts, who I spend my time with, my prayers and my worship
will be a sweet aroma unto Him. I pray that when the tears fall down my
cheeks, that I will not stay too long within my sad thoughts and that I can
keep turning my thoughts to the many, many good gifts my Father continues
to give me. I am looking forward to what is coming in this next year. I even
pray for a year of jubilee, of laughter, rejoicing, and dancing! I have hope for
even this Happy New Year!*

Carrie did indeed receive what she had hoped for: her year of
jubilee, laughing, rejoicing and dancing with Jesus! And we who
remain on this earth for a time do not grieve as those who have
no hope, for we believe that Jesus died and rose again and that
God will bring with Jesus those who have fallen asleep in Him (I
Thessalonians 4:13-14).

My walk through the valley of the shadow of death involved
grieving for the twins we lost in the pregnancy which revealed my
cancer, letting go of the prospect of bearing biological children,
and dealing with the ramifications of cancer treatment. The radical
hysterectomy took place on May 23, 1990, and I was surrounded
by wonderful friends from our church in Denver who gathered
in the hospital waiting room to pray together during my surgery.
I have an obtuse recollection of a platter of Grand Marnier-iced
cinnamon rolls from my favorite bakery beckoning to me as my
pre-op fasting self greeted those who would be praying (but not
fasting, shame on them!). I remember being led to the pre-surgical
area and lying in solitude on a gurney in the operating room before anesthesia, singing in my spirit the words of Martin Luther's
great hymn, "A Mighty Fortress is our God": "This body they
may kill; God's truth abideth still. His Kingdom is forever!" I'm
not sure the surgeon would have appreciated my sentiment, but
I know that God looks on the heart and He knew I was putting
my trust in Him.

Three weeks after surgery, and following a brief respite with
Philippe at a friend's condo in Aspen during which I climbed down

from the top of Aspen Mountain (can't keep this girl down!), I had a thought. Remembering that our church helped to support an adoption agency in Denver, Bethany Christian Services, I looked up the number in the telephone directory and put my hand on the phone. Before I could pay any heed to the fear of being rejected because I was a cancer patient, I punched in the number. A cheerful woman named Carol answered, and when I gave her my name and told her in a rather tremulous voice that my husband and I were interested in adopting a baby, she exclaimed, "I know who you are! We've been praying for you! What do you want—a boy or a girl?" No sweeter words could have met my ear; they were straight from the heart of God. Thus began the rigorous and lengthy process of applying for adoption, but it all began with hope.

Philippe and I, perhaps like many if not most prospective adoptive parents, felt an almost desperate need to prove ourselves worthy of being selected to parent a child. When one has to be fingerprinted and home-studied, there is a sense of the unnatural about the whole process; certainly labor is preferable to scrutiny (forgive me, birthmothers!). However, we held forth the continual hope that God had set us on this course and that He would fulfill the desire of our hearts. We read in Hebrews 10:35, "So do not throw away your confidence; it will be richly rewarded. You need to persevere so that when you have done the will of God, you will receive what He has promised."

Our hopes were realized on January 7, 1992, with the birth of our son, Paul Alexandre de Chambrier. Philippe and I drove through a white-out snowstorm to the United States Air Force Academy Hospital in Colorado Springs (legend has it that babies like to come during blizzards!), and when I tiptoed into his birth-mother Lisa's room, she whispered to baby Paul, "Here's your mom!" The once-bitter tears of deferred hope yielded to sobs of joy as I tenderly held our precious child for the first time. Three days later, Paul was baptized at the Air Force Academy Hospital by my father in a poignant ceremony attended by his birthmother and her family, my parents, Philippe's mother, and us. He is the perfect son for us; the one that God chose to complete our family. He is God's gift of hope.

> **Precious Lord**, You are the Help of the helpless and the God of all hope. When life seems so dim, Lord, we ask that you would renew our hope in you. I pray for all who are walking through the journey of cancer and loss, and pray that you, the God of hope, would fill them with all joy and peace as they trust in you, so that they may overflow with hope by the power of the Holy Spirit. It is in the name of Jesus that we pray, Amen.

"Hallelujah! For our Lord God Almighty reigns. Let us rejoice and be glad and give him glory! For the wedding of the Lamb has come, and his bride has made herself ready. Fine linen, bright and clean, was given her to wear." —Revelation 19:6-8

6
Godly Marriage

CARRIE

Journal entry, August 1, 2005: The Wedding of Nathan Jackson Oliver and Amy Brooke Merrell (July 15, 2005).

I will never, ever forget when Amy stepped out onto the veranda and the steps. Truly she was the most beautiful bride I had ever seen and watching Nathan's face was a moment in which God said, "This is good, and I have created this for My Glory." The wedding continued led by our dear friend Dale Schlafer. Letters were read to the parents that Nathan and Amy had written. I did cry at that one as it was such a surprise. They said their vows, they washed each other's feet as a symbol of servanthood, and they kissed each other and were presented as Mr. and Mrs. Nathan Oliver. I sat in awe the entire time. I didn't even cry much because I was in awe. In awe that I was there, in awe of two people starting their lives together and the sense of it being so right, in awe of the breeze blowing to cool us off, in awe of Brian Kemp as he sang and played his guitar with a voice so clear and so holy, in awe of God—and I knew that Glory was brought to Him on this evening of July 15, 2005.

To the Oliver family, everything in life was and is always, always, always about bringing glory to God, without qualification under any circumstances. Carrie goes on to elaborate:

I believe that in order to have hope, one needs to understand that everything we do, say, believe, pray about, exist for, is for God's glory. Only at that point do we understand what our hope exists in. Hope glorifies God. When we do not understand this, we do not have a place to put our hope. We cannot hope in ourselves, or even for ourselves. That helps me every moment I breathe because somehow when it becomes about God and not about me, there is a power that I could not ever muster up on my own. In this glorification of God, even going back to chemo after time out is about bringing glory to God as I walk through it in His name, in His power. At the end, may it bring glory to God.

The marriage relationship is a covenant relationship ordained by God between a man and a woman to bring Him glory. Godly marriage has its challenges under even normal circumstances, but is put to a severe test when one of the partners has been diagnosed with cancer. Before Philippe and I were married and in the days when I considered myself healthy as a heifer, I recall a heart to heart conversation with him in which he was trying to assess whether my love for him was truly unconditional. Looking at me with guileless, cerulean blue eyes, he asked, "Would you still love me if I were short, fat and bald?" I was a bit nonplussed at that statement and took a moment to ask the Lord to help me with my response. I then stated with confidence, "Since you are none of those things, it is really a moot point. However, I can say without a doubt that if you were to have an accident and lose a leg, or have a stroke and be disabled, I would still love you with all my heart." Little did I suspect that it would be my very own body that would present a major challenge in our lives less than two years later.

Philippe's first response to my cancer diagnosis was to turn to God and praise Him for who He is: Lord over all circumstances and the One who is able to heal all of our diseases. I leaned on him heavily for physical, mental, emotional and spiritual support every day, and he rose to the challenge again and again. I depended on

Philippe more than I ever imagined, almost with the neediness of a newborn, and he continually brought matters back to the Lord. He reminded me of the plans God had for me, to prosper and not to harm me; to give me hope and a future (Jeremiah 29:11). He shuttled me from one medical appointment to another, and then all over again. He held my hand and comforted me; he made me laugh with his silly puns. He provided emotional stability and a safe place for me to release the myriad emotions I had swirling in my head most of the time. He enthusiastically agreed to go through what seemed like an FBI interrogation in order to begin adoption proceedings after my hysterectomy. He told me I was beautiful after I fainted on the kitchen floor! He prayed without ceasing.

As we walked with Carrie and Gary through their journey with Carrie's cancer, as well as through Gary's fifth episode with oral cancer in 2006, Philippe and I saw the traits of tender love, refuge, abiding steadfastness, perseverance and bedrock faith in their marriage as well. We had the most jubilant times together in the midst of the tears and fears; truly, this was the joy of the Lord! Gary fulfilled, as does Philippe, the apostle Paul's admonition to the church in Ephesus: "Husbands, love your wives, just as Christ loved the church and gave Himself up for her to make her holy, cleansing her by the washing with water through the word, and to present her to Himself as a radiant church, without stain of wrinkle or any other blemish, but holy and blameless" (Ephesians 5:25-27). Carrie, in the midst of the ravaging cancer that was decimating her body, continued to be a supportive and godly wife to Gary, reveling in every opportunity to be together as loving spouses committed to one another and their service to the Lord.

The Olivers continued to speak at marriage conferences around the country throughout Carrie's illness. Her determination to persevere in the midst of such circumstances was in itself a testimony to Philippians 4:13, "I can do all things through Christ who strengthens me." She relates the story of the time they spoke together in Scottsdale, Arizona in August, 2005.

CARRIE

Journal entry, August, 2005: Last week as we prepared to travel to Scottsdale, I wondered if I would be able to make it. The chemo took me under or I overdid it or both, but Tuesday evening I lay on my bed and wondered how things were going to get into my suitcase, let alone carry that suitcase, get on a plane, travel and then speak. I decided that sleeping was the best option and packing in the morning was how it was going to be. Wednesday morning came and I did feel somewhat better. We packed those bags and notes and headed off on our flights to Arizona. Our arrival at the Fairmont Princess Hotel was incredible. What a beautiful place literally in the middle of the desert. Definitely a metaphor for my life: a little oasis in the middle of desert living. Our room was lovely; we unpacked and settled in and ate some food.

The next day came, the day of our workshop and our keynote. I woke very early with a two-hour time change and headed with my devotionals to the pool patio to read, pray, eat a little and watch the sun come up and talk to God about what He was going to do with me this day. The message was so clear: I was going to do a workshop and keynote with my husband in the evening. Our workshop went so great, with such sweet people in the group. It felt so "normal" and refreshing to "get" to speak with my Gary. Afterwards I rested and we began to prepare for the keynote.

Our address that evening came from some of what we have shared at other marriage workshops, but this evening we touched more upon our story as a couple and how God had been at work changing us over our 24 years and our passion for marriages to experience this change as well. It was passionate and clear and intimate and a tremendous blessing to once again be with Gary, my mate, sharing our hearts and lives with people.

The next two days, I was pretty pooped out, but what a great place to continue to rest before going to M.D. (Anderson). Both Gary and I enjoyed the people and the leaders as we spent time there. It was clear God brought us there for His purpose, His pleasure and for His glory.

As I read her words once again, I am reminded of another admonition of Paul in I Thessalonians 5:16, "Be joyful always; pray continually; give thanks in all circumstances, for this is God's will for you in Christ Jesus."

When we are yielded to His ways and promptings, God is always, without exception, glorified. I have so often thought of the integrity with which Carrie handled her physical deterioration, and how she would say, "Well, I asked God to humble me, and boy, that prayer is being answered!" Gary, still gazing on his dearly beloved wife with the eyes of a newlywed, remarked with resignation shortly before her death, "People used to stare at Carrie because she was so beautiful; now they stare at her because she's so thin." Still, he realized with every fiber of his being that one day she would have a glorious, new body, and there would be no more tears or trials. One day we will all gather at the marriage supper of the Lamb, where we will rejoice and be glad and give Him the glory!

My father, the Rev. Dr. R. Norman Herbert, was another saint who fought the good fight, finished the course and kept the faith throughout his own battle with cancer in 2001-2002. Married to my mother, Elena, for fifty-one years, Dad cherished her and expressed his own thoughts on godly marriage in this poem which he wrote in 1979:

> Godly marriage through the ages
> Joins the hearts of humankind
> To His own and one another
> In a love by Christ designed.
>
> As our Lord loved His beloved
> And did die that we might live,
> So ought Godly husbands ever
> Daily love and gladly give.
>
> As his church has loved her Savior
> With a love warm-hearted, free,
> So let each wife love her husband
> With a love that all can see.

To a world of sin and sadness,
Knowing hurt and feeling pain,
May our own sincere "I love you"
Speak a Godly message plain.[1]

Heavenly Father and Lord of all, we thank you for the gift of life and love, for the institution of marriage and the heavenly example of Christ and His bride, the Church. We stand in awe of you, Lord, and seek to glorify your name by the way in which we love those you have placed in our lives. In Jesus' name, Amen.

Everyone who is called by My name, Whom I have created for My glory; I have formed him, yes, I have made him." —Isaiah 43:7 (NKJV) Satisfy us in the morning with your unfailing love, that we may sing for joy and be glad all our days. —Psalm 90:14

7

Passion and Purpose

CARRIE
Journal entry, October 23, 2005: It is just hours away before we get on a plane to fly to Houston with the next two days full of tests, results and a doctor's consultation. I started this journal entry today with these pieces of scripture from John Piper's Don't Waste Your Life. *He says the opposite of a wasted life is to live life by a single God-exalting, soul-satisfying passion. Passion is a great word, even more so when we live it out, and live it out according to how God created for us to live. I sat in church last night once again to hear Truth speak to me. Tom Addington spoke out of John, teaching on the concept of "Jesus as the Light of the world." When we walk "with" Jesus in the light, we will never, ever be in the dark. He explained further that to walk with Jesus means something very intimate and close. It means "to follow the same road in union with Jesus Christ, in my mind, heart, with my whole life. Jesus says that whoever chooses to do so with Him, will never walk in darkness. Then it came! When we are out of union on this road of life, we are walking in darkness and walking in darkness brings us fear, anxiety and confusion. I know from my own life that getting out of union with Jesus on the road is usually subtle at first and then it goes crazy and can get very dark, very fast.*

I want to be passionate in my life. First, I want to be the person that grabs on to Jesus and walks in union with Him, heart to heart. As I get on that airplane today, I want to walk up the steps and sit in my seat with Him and if I need to lay my head on His shoulders, understand that He invites me to do so. I know He will, if I let Him, lay on that CT scan table tomorrow with me (I wish He would take the barium enema for me!). And I know that wrapping my hand in His, He will sit with me as I hear my results on Tuesday morning. To be passionate is to know the love of the Father and to choose Him in all of our circumstances because He chose us with perfect passionate love on a Cross.

Carrie had discovered the essence of her purpose in life: a passion for Jesus Christ. In *My Utmost for His Highest*, Oswald Chambers says, "There is only one relationship that matters, and that is your personal relationship to a personal Redeemer and Lord. Let everything else go, but maintain that at all costs, and God will fulfill His purpose through your life. One individual life may be of priceless value to God's purposes, and yours may be that life."[2]

When I reflect on the innumerable lives that intersected with Carrie's during the course of her illness, that statement rings true. She simply never stopped being an instrument in the hands of the Lord, even when she was so physically frail that most would have gladly relegated themselves to bed for the duration. Instead, Carrie pursued her passion, her Lord Jesus Christ, by serving Him until the end. She would ask me to pray with her for the staff members at M.D. Anderson who were caring for her, asking the Lord to bring them to a saving knowledge of Jesus Christ. She and Gary would both minister to those around them as if they were not patients themselves. Carrie finished co-authoring two books during her cancer journey and Gary told me recently that she finished her last chapter of their book *Mad About Us* just one week before she died.

I believe that it pleases the Lord immensely when our passion becomes our purpose. In eighth grade confirmation class, I memorized the Westminster Confession of Faith: "The chief end of man is to glorify God and enjoy Him forever." It made no sense to me at the time, but now it is the only thing that makes sense to me! I love the "enjoy" part! I think of the endless attributes of God and the infinite manifestations of His creativity on this beautiful earth, and I enjoy Him. I think of His mercies new every morning and His abiding faithfulness, and I enjoy Him. I think of how He has fearfully and wonderfully made each and every one of us, and I enjoy Him! I think of His neverending love, and I enjoy Him! There is no end to who God is and what He is able to do, and that includes what He desires to do through us. We read in Ephesians 2:10, "For we are God's workmanship, created in Christ Jesus to do good works, which God prepared in advance for us to do."

In December of 1995, Philippe and I were in the process of trying to adopt another child. This time the expected baby was a little girl, and we were so excited at the prospect of a sister for Paul. However, two days before Christmas, the birth mother changed her mind, and our hopes were dashed. It was like having a miscarriage or even a stillbirth, and we began yet another time of grieving.

Four months later, God's assignment of this baby girl to another couple was clarified when I was suddenly overcome by the most crushing pain imaginable in my abdomen, to the point that I was writhing in agony like a wounded animal. Nearly incoherent with pain so intense that morphine and Demerol couldn't put a dent in it, I watched the second hand on the clock over my hospital bed move round and round, wondering how many more revolutions I could endure. The baffled physicians were unable to diagnose the cause of this obtuse pain until forty hours after I had entered the hospital, and by then the situation was a life-threatening emergency. I was taken into surgery shortly after midnight on April 17, 1996. As I waited to be anesthetized, I remember praying, "Lord, I know that I may go home to be with you tonight. I'm ready—but I would like to live!" During the surgery, the doctor determined that adhesions from my cancer operation in 1990 had wrapped around the small intestine and strangulated it, resulting in diffuse peritonitis and gangrene.

When I awoke in my hospital room the next morning, my first thought was one of... great joy! I had survived! God had answered my prayer, and I was still in the land of the living! No matter that I had gadgets and do-dads connected to me every which way, a sludge jar with what looked like pond scum to drain the poison from my system, and another zipper down my abdomen even larger than the first. Ice chips for breakfast...but not for another few days? Fine with me! I was alive—and God had a new purpose for my life! I rededicated myself to Him with thanksgiving and praise.

It was about four months later that I received a totally unexpected phone call from the dean of the Shepherd School of Music at Rice University. He told me of an unanticipated, immediate faculty opening and asked if I was interested. Interested?! This was my dream job knocking at my door! I was invited to join the faculty the following week as Artist Teacher of Opera Studies. I knew, however, that my purpose was not primarily to coach singers, accompany them on the piano, and teach diction. My new purpose was to do Kingdom work on the Rice University campus! God had prepared these works in advance for me to do, and now He was calling me there for such a time as this. He was combining my passion for Jesus Christ and my purpose for living, using the gifts He had given specifically to me.

A.W. Tozer, in the anthology *Tozer on the Holy Spirit*, writes:

> The secret of a Christlike life lies partly in the deep longing for it. We grow like the ideals we admire. We reach unconsciously at last the things we aspire to. Ask God to give you a high conception of the character of Christ and an intense desire to be like Him and you will never rest until you reach your ideal.[3]

My greatest desire has become that of loving and serving the risen Christ with all of my heart, soul, mind and strength. If I keep that goal in the forefront, I cannot walk in darkness; I must walk in His light.

I found an e-mail I sent to Carrie on August 3, 2006, telling her of some additional remodeling work the Lord was doing in my life (I'm an endless construction site!). I wrote:

> I was contemplating how as frail human beings we fall from those great walls and become broken and useless, until the Master Potter picks up the pieces and refashions us in His image to be filled to the measure of all the fullness of God. What God was trying to tell me today was that I am simply that jar of clay that is only truly useful when it is filled with the Living Water. I have been struggling with wondering if I am really doing exactly what He is calling me to do and whether it's ever enough—and with the loathsome sin of comparing myself to others and coming up short. Then I fall at His feet, casting my tin crown before Him, and ask Him to fill me with all that He is so that I can bring Him glory.

The Lord went on to give me a visual image of myself as a perfume jar called "The Essence of Jan." I saw myself pouring out this jar at the feet of Jesus, and then He said, "What you have poured out, I will replace with Myself." "The Essence of Jan" was becoming the Essence of Jesus! I began to realize that He waits for us to initiate the outpouring, and then He fills us to the measure of the fullness of all that He is. I want all that He is to be poured into this jar of clay, that He might be glorified in my life, as indeed He was in the life of Carrie.

> **Dear Lord of all Creation**, You have fashioned us in your own image to bring you glory and to enjoy you forever! Thank you that you have given each one of your children a purpose that is theirs alone, and that you will lead us every step of the way in the process of fulfilling the plans you have for us. We bless your name, Lord, as you fill us with your presence. In the name of Jesus, Amen.

"Never will I leave you; never will I forsake you."
So we say with confidence, "The Lord is my helper; I will not be afraid."
—*Hebrews 13:5-6*

8

Loneliness

CARRIE
Journal entry, August 28, 2005: This has been an odd sort of couple of weeks coming home from M.D. Anderson, although I am not too surprised by some of my emotions and thoughts. The updates were so encouraging and inspiring to keep going in chemotherapy. For those that have been through chemo, you know that to be inspired to keep going is a necessity no matter the level of discomfort. There have not been highs or lows these past couple of weeks. There has been so much love and prayer and kindness and support and e-mails as the body of Christ continues to outdo itself. I know the angels are dancing and singing as they watch what Christ taught so clearly; as they see the love and faith spreading like wild flowers.

What is surprising are the incredibly lonely moments that come like waves. Loneliness is different than fear, or sadness, or depression, or anxiety. It is defined in the dictionary as "being without the company of human beings." It means being cut off from others. Let me assure you I am not cut off from others. I have precious friends calling, coming over, going places with me, sending me notes and so much more. I have people I don't know sending me notes. But something about cancer says, "I am different from you," and that puts me somewhere you are not. That is what feels lonely. If we are honest, that is what we feel when we get lonely. We feel different and cut off.

I had a doctor's appointment this past Monday with the oncologist that oversees my chemo treatment here in northwest Arkansas. I felt like a statistic in his office on Monday and walked away with the loneliness, but also thanked God for my care in Houston and the approach my physician has with me there. I praise God for that.

I can't remember when I decided to read Lance Armstrong's book, It's Not about the Bike, but I have picked it up in the last two weeks and have devoured it. I must make a confession at the risk of all you Lance groupies out there: I have not been a strong Lance fan. I mean, what is it with this guy? He divorces his wife and runs off with Sheryl Crow. Just cause she is cool and can sing?

God dealt with me on that one. One more critical, judgmental experience cleaned up in my heart. I'm still not in favor of the divorce but I have connected with Lance, the human being, and he is not that much different from me. Let me tell you about that connection. Just in the past week, a friend made a comment that has stuck deeply with me. We were talking about sin and things that were sad that were happening in people's lives and she said, "We are all just one step away from sin and evil." That same thought was reiterated at church on Saturday night as we studied the scripture in Galatians 6:1-5 on body life and restoring each other. There it was in verse 1: "And be careful not to fall into the same temptation yourself."

Reading Lance's story, the entire story of his childhood, his incredible mother and his horrendous cancer, drew me away from my loneliness and in some strange way, I have connected with Lance Armstrong rather than judged him…and it wasn't about the bike. [Carrie goes on to cite several quotes from his book.]

In this book, Lance Armstrong appears to be a man without faith in God. I HAVE GOD! I have God Almighty, Ruler of the universe and Daddy to my lonely heart. The loneliness still ebbs and flows, but reminds me more and more "Whose I am" and that there is only One that can meet my lonely needs anyway.

Thank you, God, for these last two weeks in this journey and for Lance Armstrong: a vibrant, courageous survivor of cancer and winner of many *races—and who would be an incredible witness in your kingdom, bringing you glory if he knew you. I pray for that.*

Carrie's thoughts on loneliness led me to reflect on my own, particularly during my own cancer experience. I definitely felt different from others and was especially aware of it when I would encounter expectant women or new mothers. I recall being with Philippe on our little retreat to Aspen three weeks after my hysterectomy, and being seated in the Chart House restaurant looking at the menu when an about-to-pop pregnant woman walked in and started to chat with the waitress about her obvious condition. My emotions flooded to the surface and overwhelmed me to the extent that I blurted out to Philippe, "I've gotta get out of here!" Despite my dear husband's presence, I felt so very much alone, so different. Denied entrance to the Pregnancy Party; admitted to the Cancer Club. Not knowing another woman who really understood how I felt at that moment.

I don't know if Carrie ever specifically prayed for God to send her a friend who would understand intimately what she was enduring, but He knew her needs and worked through the Rev. Stew Grant to fulfill Carrie's unspoken request. I had not a moment's hesitation when Stew asked me in December of 2005 to come alongside Carrie and be her friend when she came to Houston for treatments at M.D. Anderson. I knew that it was a Kingdom assignment; I just never realized how it would also transform and bless my own life beyond measure!

After sending Andrew Oliver a gift for his eighteenth birthday several months after Carrie died, something perhaps an aunt would do, I was touched when Andrew asked his dad, "What was Mom's friendship with Jan about?" Gary responded, "It was like a divinely pre-ordained sisterhood." I asked Gary to elaborate on this because I didn't trust my own objectivity in assessing my friendship with Carrie; perhaps she just had an amazing gift for loving all of the people in her life and making them feel uniquely valued. However,

Gary felt that God had called me to be a Barnabas, an encourager, to Carrie for several reasons: I took prayer very seriously; I spoke a "language" very similar to hers; I had a call from God to minister to her, but she could also feel free to minister to me; I was living in Houston and made myself available to her. Gary further explained that Carrie sensed a sovereign synergy in our relationship, as though God had arranged for us to have a sister in each other. He laughingly said, "She felt like you were from the same tribe!" He added, "Carrie would refer to you as 'My Jan' and felt that through you, there was an intentional manifestation of Jesus; that she was not forgotten. The two of you experienced a deeper friendship in a year and a half than many people ever do."

Imagine that! God, in His manifold and mysterious ways, provided not only an encourager for Carrie during the greatest trial of her life, but a synergistic sister for me in the aftermath of the tragic death by suicide of my own sister, Jennifer. I hadn't asked for God to provide this relationship for me, either, but He knew what I needed because He knows my needs better than I know them myself. God, in His grace, did exceedingly abundantly more than I could ask or even imagine (Ephesians 3:20). He supplied all of my need according to His riches in glory in Christ Jesus (Philippians 4:19).

Even though Carrie is no longer physically here, she remains in my heart forever and has made an indelible impact on who I am and on how I love others. I miss her presence but know the person of Jesus more because of His love so bountifully manifested in Carrie.

I think that Jesus sometimes felt alone, too. There were times He chose to be by Himself: "After He had dismissed them, He went up into the hills by Himself to pray" (Matthew 14:23). This was when He spent time with the Father, refreshing Himself. He was certainly not lonely. But in order to fulfill God's plan for redemption, He had to be separated from His Father. He took on Himself the sin of the world, so for a time, there was a chasm between them. I picture my Savior on the cross at Calvary, surrounded by a jeering crowd and a few loyal followers, and asking, "My God, my God, why have you forsaken me?" The One without sin became sin for you and for me. That was the ultimate loneliness.

We are only sojourners, pilgrims in this world, and we soon whither like grass, but our promise is in the heavenly realm for all eternity. During the Last Supper, Jesus was preparing the disciples for His death and assuring them that He was not leaving them alone. I like Eugene Peterson's rendering of the passage from John 14:25-27 in *The Message*:

> I'm telling you these things while I'm still living with you. The Friend, the Holy Spirit whom the Father will send at my request, will make everything plain to you. He will remind you of all the things I have told you. I'm leaving you well—whole. That's my parting gift to you. Peace. I don't leave you the way you're used to being left—feeling abandoned, bereft. So don't be upset. Don't be distraught.[4]

As Carrie shared in her journal, feeling lonely has to do with "being cut off." When we know Jesus, we have the assurance of His presence and the knowledge that the Comforter will meet those needs that no human being can satisfy. Jesus continued to tell the disciples at the Last Supper, "I am the vine; you are the branches. If a man remains in me and I in him, he will bear much fruit; apart from me, you can do nothing" (John 15:5). If we abide in Christ, and are not "cut off" from the Vine, we have the assurance that there will be much fruit.

Carrie's life bore fruit: more bushel baskets than anyone could possibly count. She allowed the Master Gardener to prune her as she abided in Him, and she brought the Father glory. Because of her life, many know Jesus, and because He lives, we will have His abiding presence and love forever! This makes me think of the great old hymn, "Abide with Me" by William H. Monk:

Abide with me—fast falls the eventide;
The darkness deepens—Lord, with me abide;
When other helpers fail and comforts flee,
Help of the helpless, O abide with me!

I need Thy presence every passing hour—
What but Thy grace can foil the tempter's power?
Who like Thyself my guide and stay can be?
Thru cloud and sunshine, O abide with me!

Precious Lord, You are the One who will never leave us or forsake us; our Refuge; our Shelter; our Hiding Place. You are the good Shepherd who cradles your lambs in your arms. You are the Vine in which we abide with confidence, knowing that in you, we will bear much fruit. Thank you that you have gone before us to prepare a place for us; that where you are, we may be also. In Jesus' name, Amen.

For it is by grace you have been saved, through faith—and this is not from yourselves, it is the gift of God—not by works, so that no one can boast. For we are God's handiwork, created in Christ Jesus to do good works, which God prepared in advance for us to do. —Ephesians 2:8-10

9

Gifts

J esus says in Matthew 24:35, "Heaven and earth will pass away, but my words will never pass away." The only things we will carry with us from life on earth when we die are those things of eternal value: our relationship with Jesus Christ; the Word of God that has been hidden in our hearts; our relationships with those that God has placed in each of our lives. Nothing else has any lasting value. All are gifts from our heavenly Father.

CARRIE

Journal entry, September 27: I have thought much about "gifts" this week. I believe these thoughts are with me for a couple of reasons, because so many gifts have come my way and because I finished reading The Life of the Beloved *by Henri Nouwen. He says this about giving: "We become beautiful people when we give whatever we can give: a smile, a handshake, a kiss, an embrace, a word of love, a present, a part of our life…all of our life."[5]*

I woke up one morning to find mums and pumpkins all over my front porch. Two lovely people decided to decorate my porch for Fall! That doesn't even get done at my house when I am well! A container of tea, an e-mail, a hug, a look of love, a soft word, honest compassion, a meal brought, a phone call with concern…and of course, a prayer pager that goes off every five minutes or so…..I like, as well, the thought from Nouwen that says, "The real gifts we give come from who we are rather than what we give." That thought exhorts me. I am accountable to that thought, that truth. I pray more and more that I am a broken person that is offering sweet gifts of who God is making me to be. That is hard in the midst of such incredible weakness.

What was evident in Carrie to all who knew her was the richness of God's love being poured out of her through the gifts He had placed and cultivated in her, even and perhaps especially in the midst of her weakness. When she was weak, Christ was strong. Paul talks about spiritual gifts in his first letter to the Corinthian church, chapter 12: "There are different kinds of gifts, but the same Spirit. There are different kinds of working, but the same God works all of them in all men." Carrie's particular gifts were many: serving, teaching, leadership, exhortation, compassion, wisdom, faith, hospitality…and on and on. It was so beautiful to see her gifts increase even as her body diminished. She served her Lord even with her last breath, and she glorifies Him even now with the legacy she has left.

I have always been a gift-giver, delighting in the surprise on the face of the intended recipient, and joyful in the knowledge that I had expressed my love in this way. It was really after I met Carrie, however, that I began to see my perspective change on this. The truth is, I never quite felt that any gift I gave was adequate enough. No matter how much time and effort I expended on making or finding the "perfect" gift, I always felt as if there was something lacking. What I learned through my friendship with Carrie is that she valued much more greatly the gift of time together than any material offering. Perhaps because she had been told that her days were numbered, God's gift of life and this short time on earth took on a greater significance. She prized the times we sat together praying as we waited for test results; she delighted in coming up to The Woodlands and having a sleepover during some of her M.D.

Anderson visits; she so enjoyed an outdoor picnic lunch at Whole Foods or a fragrant cup of Starbucks together; she loved getting together as a foursome with our husbands. One of her greatest gifts to me was a line from a note she had written to me: "You are a gift of God and through this cancer I received you!" God gave both of us priceless gifts of eternal value through this friendship.

Another gift of friendship that originated with a cancer diagnosis is with PJ, a woman who started coming to the healing service at our church after being diagnosed with brain cancer in 2003. As we prayed together during these monthly services, I was encouraged in my own faith through PJ's testimony of God's faithfulness and the gift of perseverance He is working out in her, and our relationship as prayer partners grew into a friendship. PJ's writing reminds me a bit of Carrie's in her ability to uncover and express so succinctly the emotions we have when confronted with the prospect of diminishing time on earth. She shared her thoughts on the gift of time in an e-mail from April 21, 2007—the date that would have been Carrie's fiftieth birthday:

> Time….Why is it when we stop and think about the time that has gone by, we remember so quickly the dates of bad or unpleasant situations that happened in our lives? I started thinking about the last ten years of my own life. I admit the things that came to my mind were not the good and happy remembrances, but the negative. I have been divorced almost ten years, had cancer almost six years, and been unable to work for over three years. You get the picture. These were the first thoughts that came to my recollection: I wondered why it is that the mind can recall dates of personal tragedies, heartbreaks, and painful situations so quickly, yet in the same time span, so much good has also taken place. I would like to try re-programming my mind to be able to recall the good things first; to be able to overshadow the bad ones, but not to completely

forget them. I know some of them have caused me to grow and to be a stronger person. In my last ten years, I have met people who have become dear and lifelong friends. I have seen precious babies born. I have seen children grow up into amazing young adults. I have seen couples fall in love and watched them get married. I have traveled to other countries and seen amazing landscapes. I have learned to enjoy some of life's simplest pleasures, like watching and listening to the birds sing, looking at beautiful flowers, and even watching the cars go by.

Jim Croce sang a song many years ago called "Time in a Bottle." As I thought about the lyrics, I asked myself what I would do if I could actually put time into a bottle. After a bit of thought, I believe I would want to put my future in the bottle. I would want to do away with the worries of tomorrow. I would try to live my life for the day that I had just been given. I would try to practice a system or plan. I would call it the "more or less of." It would go something like this: I want to be more grateful and less expecting. I want to see the good in others, and be less judgmental. I want to be more attentive to others' needs and less aware of my own. I want to be more gracious and less demanding. I want to be more generous and less selfish. I want to be more patient and less stressed. I want to spend more time with friends and less time on excuses. I want to be more encouraging and less critical. I want to give more smiles and fewer frowns. There are endless "more or less of" possibilities!

So today, I am hypothetically putting my future into the bottle. I want to start putting the "more or less of" plan into action right now and stop waiting for tomorrow. I want the world to be a better place and

I want to be a better person. I know a simple change in my outlook can help. So, if you could put time in a bottle, what would you put in yours?

The apostle Paul offers what I would choose as my answer to PJ's question: "If you could put time in a bottle, what would you put in yours?" The words are in Colossians 1:27, "Christ in you, the hope of glory." What I want in my bottle is the full measure of Christ. In II Corinthians 4:7, Paul says:

> We have this treasure in jars of clay to show that this all-surpassing power is from God and not from us. We are hard-pressed on every side, but not crushed; perplexed, but not in despair; persecuted, but not abandoned; struck down, but not destroyed. We always carry around in our body the death of Jesus so that the life of Jesus may also be revealed in our body.

I want my time in this bottle, this jar of clay, to be His time.

God desires for each of His children to use the gifts He has imparted for eternal purpose. When our son Paul was seven, he wanted a new and improved, way-cool bicycle in the worst way. Philippe and I offered to meet him halfway if he would save his allowance and birthday money. When that auspicious day arrived, they trekked off to Wal-Mart and returned a bit later with a shiny purple two-wheeler. After a few spins down the street and back, Paul came in and turned on a Christian television program. Seeing a commercial for a children's mission fund showing impoverished children in Third World countries, he suddenly began to weep. He cried out, "Mom! Take that bike back and send all the money to these children!" My heart nearly burst with joy at the knowledge that God had planted in Paul the seeds of compassion and gift-giving. This led to the sponsorship of several children through Compassion International, one of whom we visited in Uganda last year. We were then able to start a program called "The Uganda Book Project" to provide books to children that Compassion serves in this beleaguered country. God used Paul's gifts to provide His gifts to others.

The author of *The Pilgrim's Progress*, John Bunyan, was a seventeenth-century believer who was imprisoned for twelve years for preaching without a license. While incarcerated, he wrote his autobiography entitled *Grace Abounding to the Chief of Sinners*. In an excerpt from this, he speaks of exercising the gift of preaching that God had given to him:

> I began to see that the Holy Spirit never intended that people who had gifts and abilities should bury them in the earth, but rather, He commanded and stirred up such people to the exercise of their gift and sent out to work those who were able and ready. And so, although I was the most unworthy of all the saints, I set upon this work. Though trembling, I used my gift to preach the blessed gospel, in proportion to my faith, as God had showed me in the holy Word of truth. When the word got around that I was doing this, people came in by the hundreds from all over to hear the word preached. At first, I could hardly believe that God would speak through me to the heart of anyone, and I still counted myself unworthy. Yet those who were quickened through my preaching loved me and had a respect for me…And when I saw that they were beginning to live differently, and that their hearts were eagerly pressing after the knowledge of Christ and rejoicing that God sent me to them, then I began to conclude that God had blessed His work through me. And so I rejoiced.[6]

Our gracious heavenly Father, You have given to us the greatest Gift ever given: your Son, our Savior and Lord, Jesus Christ. You have given us the gift of life on earth so that we can come to know you, glorify you, and enjoy you forever! Thank you that every good and perfect gift is from you, and that you have given us the opportunity to use everything for your everlasting glory. May it be so. In Jesus' name, Amen.

I know what it is to be in need, and I know what it is to have plenty. I have learned the secret of being content in any and every situation, whether well fed or hungry, whether living in plenty or in want. I can do all this through him who gives me strength. —Philippians 4:12-13

10

Reality

C ARRIE
Journal entry, July 9, 2005: I thought much about "reality" this week. You see, at heart I am a contemplative. That is a very fancy way of saying I think a lot. Sometimes thinking is helpful and sometimes it isn't because contemplatives have a tendency to go down funky roads of depression and then they have to get back on the right path again. When things are not "normal" feeling in life, one can question "reality." Sometimes real is good and sometimes real does not feel good. In the children's book The Velveteen Rabbit, *the bunny goes through hardships and rejection and bumps and scrapes in order to become real. The Velveteen Rabbit is not your "normal" stuffed animal.*

I dropped a dear friend of mine off at the airport this week. I watched her beautiful, smiling face; her spring in her step. I thought of her life she was going to: a loving husband, and a daughter soon to be married. Her life is very different from mine right now. I thought about how healthy she looked and how fun it was to have her visit for one precious day. I knew that she was real and our time was real. I then began to drive down the road to home and noticed and enjoyed the sunny day and the green fields and trees and I knew that the day was "real." I then let my thoughts turn for moments to "me" and my cancer and then things began to feel "unreal." Loss, death, hurts, illness are all examples of what causes us to question reality and we long for something that feels normal and known and good. The tears began to drip down my cheeks. I know that the Velveteen Rabbit had his moments, too, on his way to real. I picked that book back up and for now he is my hero. He didn't give up. He wanted to be real more than normal and he fought to be so.

My reality is what I am living, and who the heck knows what normal is. I know I can't think about it long, or entertain the thoughts that everyone else has normal and what I have is reality. This past Friday after three counseling sessions, I was scheduled to run up to Highlands Oncology in Rogers for a blood draw to check my levels before leaving for Florida and the wedding. I never go to this clinic. I always go to Fayetteville, as it is closer to Siloam. The Fayetteville clinic is where all of my blood work is done and my treatments take place, but because I was already at the church seeing clients, I was closer to Rogers. I had about a forty-five minute slot before I had to be back in Siloam Springs. I walked in, sat down, and then was called to get the draw. I came back out to wait for the results. A beautiful young woman spoke to me and said, "You are the one with the website." I said, "Yes! How did you know?" and she explained her connection. I knew of her cancer and her battle of it coming back. I looked at her with tears in my eyes and told her to hang on, and to believe, and she said some precious things to me and we hugged. I left wondering what God was up to as He so evidently had us meet. I don't exactly know that answer, but I know it was "real." I am praying for you, Sonia.

I think that one of the reasons Carrie and I were such close friends was the "contemplative" aspect in both of us that relentlessly searched for deeper meaning and significance. This journal entry takes me back to my own cancer diagnosis and treatment, when I would often furtively glance at the faces of other women in the supermarket and wonder if they had any idea of how gut-wrenchingly painful life could be. I found myself growing impatient with friends who would complain about mundane things like their haircuts or their children's slovenly table manners or their husbands' excessive workloads. But over time, I became aware that there were many more who, although they wore a façade of normalcy, were walking in shoes similar to mine and were sharing my version of reality. As Carrie did with Sonia, I sought out these women, and many became my friends. There was a bond that transcended the normal criteria for choosing friends: we were all walking through the cancer experience. We were all learning to live life to the fullest, not in spite of it—but because of it.

Jesus said, "I have come that they may have life, and have it abundantly" (John 10:10). I used to think that abundant life was the world's concept of "the good life": a happy marriage, a few intelligent children, an interesting profession, lots of friends. What I hadn't factored in was that we don't live in fictitious and idealistic Lake Woebegone; we live in a world where there is good and there is evil. Despite our best intentions, we will all encounter elements of both and suffer the consequences of living in a fallen world. Sometimes these repercussions are the result of our own poor choices; sometimes they are inexplicable. Jesus said in John 16:33, "In this world you will have trouble. But take heart! I have overcome the world." Abundant life is life that is lived with and for Christ.

CARRIE

Journal entry, July 3, 2005: I will never forget the morning I awoke this week dreaming and then remembering the dream so vividly. I was in a church just about ready to give a message (That right there is very memorable, since I really don't do that sort of thing!). The words of John 3:16 were coming out of my mouth. Most of us know it well: "For God so loved the world that He gave His only begotten Son, so that everyone who believes in Him will not perish but have eternal life." The message that I was dreaming that I was about to give is that God also sent His Son that we might have life right "now," in the very present of our ordinary day, not just in eternity, and that most of us need to ask what that means to us today. We have the gift of life.

A friend asked the question this week, "What is the difference between walking life with cancer or without it?" I wonder if the question is more, "Are we walking in a way that says we are 'alive'?"— alive because we have

God's only begotten Son walking with us, breathing through us, and able to make each day deeply better than survival. Living that way transcends every experience of the day: cancer, lists, deadlines, demands, limitations, things that often suck the living life right out of us.

I went on to read in Henri Nouwen that same morning (funny how God when He is working ties things together so neatly if we are watching), and he writes about how we must keep our eyes fixed on the prize. What is the prize? It is the divine life, the eternal life, the life with and in God; and that wondering what it will be like after I die is only a distraction from the clear goal that is reachable right now, right where I am, because eternal life is life in and with God, and God is where I am here and now.

That same prize is what the apostle Paul is referring to in I Corinthians 9:24-25, "Run in such a way as to get the prize. Everyone who competes in the games goes into strict training. They do it to get a crown that will not last; but we do it to get a crown that will last forever." In many ways, being faced with a trial like cancer forces one to confront these matters and decide whether to succumb to the present difficult circumstances, or to walk through them with the One who has overcome the world and with whom we will spend eternity. When we choose to live abundantly with Christ in the midst of such a trial, He completely changes our perspective. Life becomes fuller; every experience is heightened.

My father was diagnosed with inoperable metastatic prostate cancer in December of 2001. Having served in the ministry for forty years, he had encountered many scenarios like this with parishioners and even family. Somehow all the rules change when it is oneself who receives the diagnosis. I told my mom that I would stay with Dad that night in the hospital, and I prayed throughout the sleepless hours for the words to tell Dad that he would soon die. Around five the next morning, I felt that the Lord had sufficiently prepared me, and I tiptoed gingerly to the side of his bed and said very tremulously, "Dad, would you like for me to tell you what they found, or would you rather wait for the doctor?" He said, "No, I'd like for you to tell me." I was weeping by this time, trying to coherently read a passage of scripture to him, when he said, "Jannie, you're just like me. You cry at beautiful things." He made it so easy for me to tell him that he would soon be in the eternal presence of God!

The last five months of my dad's life were perhaps the most fruitful of all. He met with each of his four children to give his blessing and to exhort us to walk closely with Jesus; he finished writing a book of hymns and poems that had been on the back burner for too long; he met with countless friends and church members to encourage them in their faith and to assure them that there was no fear in dying when one is in Christ. Dad ministered to the staff of the hospice where he lived the last three weeks, with my dear mother by his side most of the time. They were even asked to make a video on behalf of the hospice, during which my dad shared his thoughts on dying as a believer. In his withered physical state, with his once-resonant bass voice reduced to a throaty whisper, I remember him saying with the utmost confidence, "It's really rather a glorious thing to die." And I believe that it is, for my Father has told me so! "To live is Christ; to die is gain" (Philippians 1:2).

> **Gracious Lord**, we rejoice that you have overcome the world; that our present sufferings are not worth comparing to the joy that will be revealed in eternity. Thank you that you will walk with us through these trials and that we can be content and even joyful in the midst of them, knowing that you will abide with us always. We pray in Jesus' name, Amen.

Brothers and sisters, I do not consider myself yet to have taken hold of it. But one thing I do: Forgetting what is behind and straining toward what is ahead, I press on toward the goal to win the prize for which God has called me heavenward in Christ Jesus. —Philippians 3:13-14

11

Perseverance

Persistence and perseverance are two very different things. Both imply tenacity: keeping on "keeping on." But persistence carries with it the implication of self-will, while perseverance connotes a calling. I have always been a persistent individual, sometimes to the point of compulsion. When I was a freshman piano major at Northwestern University, my professor entered me in the Society of American Musicians competition in Chicago, and I practiced for months in preparation for this event. Since I was among the youngest contenders, I had a certain amount of apprehension about all of this, so my mom drove in to take me to the competition and sit in the audience.

The first piece I played was the fugue from Bach's e-minor *Toccata*, and I got off to a great start. However, my mind became distracted and I soon lost my way in the subject of that fugue. Wishing that someone would drop some breadcrumbs on those piano keys to help me find my way, I repeated and repeated the section like a mouse in a maze. Finally, one of the judges said, "Miss, would you please go on to the next piece?" Reluctantly, I submitted to his request, played the Chopin flawlessly—and was disqualified from the competition because of my memory loss. I just didn't want to give up! That was persistence, tenacity, or just plain stubbornness, not perseverance. And boy was I thankful my mom was there to help me pick up the pieces!

This past semester at Rice University, I had to play several recitals for the singers that I coach. I had been diagnosed in early January with two disk herniations in my lower lumbar spine, and was experiencing an increase in pain in late March and early April. However, I felt called to complete the work that I had promised to fulfill and which was a requirement for my students to complete their degrees. The very last recital of the season was on April 22, and I was in such abject agony that I could hardly walk. My dear Philippe offered to drive me to Rice (we live an hour away) and we beseeched God through praise for strength. Always true to His word, God supplied what I needed, and instead of Philippe having to carry me on and off stage, he sat in the audience and prayed! That, to me, exemplifies perseverance: the pressing on towards a goal to which one has been called, trusting in His strength and not our own.

The Bible is full of examples of those who persevered because they were called by God: Abraham, Noah, Moses, Nehemiah, Job, David, Paul, Peter, John; these are just a few. They were all at various times, and some of them many times, in situations where God led them to persevere for a cause to which He had called them. Most of them would probably not have chosen that particular path, but God had a greater purpose in mind. As Isaiah 55:8 says, "For my thoughts are not your thoughts; neither are your ways my ways," declares the Lord. And so it was with Carrie: one who trusted in the Lord, was called to a purpose, and would not give up. Ever.

CARRIE

Journal entry, September 22, 2006: On "Not Giving Up!"

For some reason, this phrase has been with me this entire past week. I have been thinking about what type of person I am when it comes to "giving up" and how I have dealt with situations in the past which offered me the choice of "giving up." Have you ever thought about "giving up?" Have you given up on something? We can experience "giving up" in such a wide variety of scenarios: might be a relationship, might be a job, the pursuit of a dream, on life, a race, on God, on self, on hope, on heaven, and yes—even in illness. I see it in my work with clients at the counseling office. There are those that are downcast and hopeless and they give up, and then there are those that are willing to stick it out, persevere, even for a lifetime. They don't "give up."

I think about this whole thing because, yes, in illness, on the days of weariness, a bad digestive system, fatigue because of anemia, not being able to play tennis, run, or walk the four miles I used to walk, having to say no to some social events, looking at the scale and not seeing any progress with pounds, noticing the hair is thinning again, missing friends, wanting to be someone else that does not have cancer (as someone said to me, unzip my body and climb into another!)—a small thought of waving the white flag sounds okay.

Then I think, well, what does that mean? Renouncing all that I believe? No. Not getting up in the morning? No. Discontinuing chemotherapy? No. And I realize that that is a most unhelpful thought. So what have I done with this in the past? I don't think I've given up much in my lifetime. There have been times when the fear prevented me from trying. I think playing golf a couple of weeks ago was a demonstration of not giving up. I gave up on the first hole to restructure my mind and get set again and tell my body it was going to do this, and then I enjoyed the silly game. I don't think I ever quit a race in track or quit a class in school, and I certainly will not quit on my husband, as different from me as he is! I won't quit on my kids; I believe in them and they need to be believed in, but what does it mean to not give up in the midst of illness?

I know people do. And let me say that giving up is different from feeling led to let go of treatment and die with dignity. I think there are two keys here when it comes to giving up. First, each day is a gift from God, and He promises to walk with us in that day, so why give up if He is carrying us anyway? Secondly, we are called to persevere. I don't think it is denial to want to live and to believe that God has life for us. I still believe He is sovereign and

He will have His way with me, but I am not "giving up" on what I believe is His hand on my life, every moment of it, even the hard and difficult and the "want-to-give-up-thoughts" times. So after thinking about the "not giving up" verses, I choose to not give up.

I will greet each day, even after cranky moments and the feelings that nobody should have to be on chemo this long, with perseverance and a belief that God will give me strength to "not give up," and in this process, there are seeds sown: there is potential increasingly deeper intimacy with Him, and there are the reviving nutrients of His Word. I Timothy 6:11 talks about the godly life that is one of perseverance as well as faith, love and gentleness. Isn't that interesting? To not give up will require perseverance, faith, love and gentleness. A dear friend of mine gave me one of those little biblical name cards a couple of weeks ago. It says "Carrie" and underneath my name is the word "Strong." Yep, I knew that, and strong-willed is what I have been in the past, but now I know that "not giving up" and strength really are coupled with such precious attributes as a humble gentleness, faith and love mixed with courage. It takes courage to keep going. It takes courage to fight the battle, and you have to have a sense of what you are fighting for. I know what I am fighting for: I am fighting to be a witness, to sow seeds, to reap a harvest, to hold my grandchildren, to protect my children from grief and sorrow, to live with my mate, to run again and to praise God from the depths of my heart for a long, long time. I can't give up; too much to fight for.

I am a woman who, in her humanness, is very afraid, is sick, is weak and has no courage or strength. In my Lord Jesus Christ, I am a woman whose name means "Strong." I have faith, a sense of what I am fighting for, and I have His arms to carry me. I also have the body of Christ which has not "Given Up On Me!" Oh, thank you from every corner of my heart. No matter what, this will be a battle that is won.

Gary Oliver would often end our prayer times or conversations with the words, "More than conquerors!" He was quoting from Paul's letter to the Romans, chapter 8:35-39:

> Who shall separate us from the love of Christ? Shall trouble or hardship or persecution or famine or naked-

ness or danger or sword? As it is written: "For your sake we face death all day long; we are considered as sheep to be slaughtered." No, in all these things we are MORE THAN CONQUERORS through Him who loved us. For I am convinced that neither death nor life, neither angels nor demons, neither the present nor the future, nor any powers, neither height nor depth, nor anything else in all creation, will be able to separate us from the love of God that is in Christ Jesus our Lord.

Gary sent both Philippe and me copies of a real jewel of a book, *Secrets of the Secret Place*, by Bob Sorge. In the chapter called "The Secret of Enduring," he writes of the Scriptures as being his source of constancy; that God reveals Himself to those who persevere. He goes on to tell of the biblical symbolism of the pearl, which is formed inside an oyster through an intruding grain of sand trapped within its shell. The resultant prize of the pearl represents the refinement that God is working within us through hardship. He writes:

> The formative value of tribulation is sometimes directly proportional to the duration of the crucible. The longer the distress, the more valuable the pearl. It is the confidence of this reality which empowers us to persevere with joy. When we endure in love through hardship, we qualify to enter the gates of pearl—for the only way to enter the eternal city is through the pearly gates of "treasure perfected in hardship."[7]

Carrie ran with perseverance the course that the Lord set before her. She fought the good fight, finished the course and kept the faith. She entered those pearly gates of "treasure perfected in hardship" and is living abundant eternal life with the Pearl of great price. She persevered—and won the Prize!

Our dear heavenly Father, You have called each one of us to your purpose and it is only by your grace that we stand. Give us the strength to persevere in faith, with love and gentleness in all circumstances, as you conform us to the image of your Son, Jesus Christ. Help us to live as more than conquerors, knowing that nothing can ever separate us from your love. In Jesus' name we pray, Amen.

Put on the full armor of God, so that you can take your stand against the devil's schemes. For our struggle is not against flesh and blood, but against the rulers, against the authorities, against the powers of this dark world and against the spiritual forces of evil in the heavenly realms.
—*Ephesians 6:11-12*

12

Lies of the Enemy

I sent Carrie an e-mail on August 15, 2006:

Sweet, dear Carrie:

Ever since reading your e-mail this morning in which you mentioned your battle with fear, I have been praying for the words to share with you. As I've told you before, the fear I faced after my own cancer diagnosis and treatment was more ominous and "life-threatening" than the cancer itself. It was only when Philippe gently confronted me with reminders of God's sovereignty and perfect provision every step of the way that I was able to lay aside that fear.

Carrie, fear is never, ever from God; it is only a lie of the enemy. Just as the symptoms lie, so does the manifestation of the fear. It becomes a "god" when our focus turns to it and indulges it. The only antidote is praise to the one and true God who alone is able to overcome it. A verse that has spoken to me so often is Psalm 8:2, "From the lips of children and infants you have ordained praise because of your enemies, to silence the foe and the avenger." It is the act of recognizing that fear is a lie, holding the thought captive, and consciously deciding to praise God rather than indulge the fear. Then that fear must be banished, because perfect love casts out fear.

As I prayed, I sensed the Lord impressing on me three words: Reject, Rejoice, and Receive. You must REJECT the lies of the enemy, REJOICE in the Lord always, and RECEIVE the gift of healing that He wants to bring to you. Think of the countless ways in which God has protected you so far, dear one. He will be the same every step of the way! He has imparted so much of Himself to you over the past fifteen months that you are indeed a new creation! Now He wishes to complete the process because He desires for you to be whole. Perhaps He allows our physical illnesses so that the greater diseases, such as fear in your case and mine, can be submitted to Him and conquered! We offer all of ourselves to Him, and He cleans us up—lock, stock, and barrel!

Carrie, I relate so closely to you and only offer what I myself have battled and seen firsthand. God is faithful and I am standing with you in expectancy to see what He will do. I am praying that during the next (almost) four weeks until your appointment at M.D. Anderson, He will be restoring your body to health. Specifically, I am asking that the tumor on your pancreas and whatever is on your spine would continue to be incinerated and disappear, that the fluid in your abdomen would dissipate, and that you would gain weight so that you are 111 pounds when they weigh you in September. Mind you, I have never prayed for a friend to gain weight, as most would hate me for it! You're the exception, dear Carrie…but then you're exceptional in every way!

Trust in the Lord with all of your heart, Carrie, and lean not unto your own understanding. Praise Him all the day long; rejoice in the Lord always!

FEAR NOT, for He is with you! I love you so.

Jan

We read in Luke 10:17-20 of Jesus appointing and sending out seventy-two believers with the impartation of His authority to heal the sick and cast out demons. They returned with joy and said:

"Lord, even the demons submit to us in your name." He replied, "I saw Satan fall like lightning from heaven. I have given you authority to trample on snakes and scorpions and to overcome all the power of the enemy; nothing will harm you. However, do not rejoice that the spirits submit to you, but rejoice that your names are written in heaven."

That became a verse I would share with Carrie many times over the following months and one that I am continually drawing on in the present. We often spoke of the sneaky means Satan would use to interject his agenda into our thoughts in seemingly innocuous ways: articles on cancer statistics in doctors' offices; the cryptic looks on the faces of technicians as they performed CT scans or ultrasounds; well-meaning friends who would say things like, "Oh, you've lost weight, haven't you!" as they hugged us; persistent symptoms that relentlessly reminded us that our bodies were not healthy. After indulging our flesh in the misery of anxiety and despair, we would remember that God is in charge, and the Holy Spirit would help us to turn our attention away from the master deceiver and father of all lies and focus on our Lord Jesus, the Author and Finisher of our faith. Rarely did we linger too long on the intensity of the spiritual battle; we fixed our thoughts on the One who has overcome evil and allowed Him to continue to transform us by the renewing of our minds.

CARRIE

Journal entry, June 12, 2006: There is always a battle, isn't there? The Word speaks of this truth. Satan is prowling around seeking the next person he wants to devour. As Matt and I drove home, many of my thoughts turned to this cancer battle. I am tired of the battle; not waving a white flag but more like running a race where the laps in between are the hardest to run. I have run a 10K and found the middle to last miles are so hard. You have to work on the thought, "Am I going to make it?" I told Wendy last night after church that I have struggled with wondering if people are tired of this cancer like me. Will they still be there? These are the thoughts that Satan plants: "You are alone; you won't make it; your God will let you down; what do you really have to live for anyway?" Church was water for my thirsty spirit last night. We worshiped and praised and I listened to truth, and Satan's whispering lies went away.

James 4:7-8 tells us, "Submit yourselves then to God. Resist the devil, and he will flee from you." Not just skulk away like a dejected dog…but flee! I like that. I have found time and again that he just can't stand it when we praise God. He particularly detests our singing God's praises, so that's one that we use in our household a lot! When I could hardly walk and was writhing in pain from my ruptured disk, Philippe put on (very, very loud!) praise music and we began singing "Thou, O Lord, are a Shield for me; my Glory and the Lifter of my head!" And the accuser would flee.

We as Christians need to remember that the death and resurrection of Jesus won the battle. It is finished! God has already won the victory and has limited the extent of Satan's power. We have been given spiritual armor to protect us from the enemy. When I arise in the morning, and before I do anything else, I put on the whole armor of God (Ephesians 6:14-17). I like to dress myself from the top down, so I start with the helmet of salvation to protect my thoughts. Then I put on the breastplate of righteousness to remind me that Jesus' robe of righteousness guards my viscera, the center of my emotions; next comes the belt of truth: that Jesus Himself is the Way, the Truth and the Life; then I put on the shoes of the readiness of the gospel of peace to prepare myself to walk in His ways and take them to this world in need; I pick up the shield of faith, with which to deflect the fiery darts of the enemy; and finally, I wield the sword of the Spirit: the Word of God, which is quick and powerful and sharper than any double-edged sword. Only then can I begin my day.

I think that the enemy, being the prince of darkness, takes special delight in tormenting us at night. Fears seem to loom larger; pain is especially intense; doubts creep in uninvited. When Philippe is traveling, which is predictably often since he is a pilot, I have found that the best remedy for this is to speak an authority prayer out loud over our home and each one of us. I say something like, "This home and territory belongs only to the Lord Jesus Christ, who has all authority here. Satan has NO authority here, and in the name of Jesus, I command him and his minions to flee." I am also a tremendous advocate of Christian radio, and keep KHCB, which stands for Keeping Him Close By, on low volume throughout the night. Not only does it chase away the enemy, but there have been countless times when the Holy Spirit has nudged me awake just in time to hear a song, scripture verse, or sermon that would minister in exactly the way I needed at that particular moment. God is always faithful. He draws near to us when we draw near to Him.

One of the books that Gary and Carrie read at about the same time as Philippe and I was *The Supernatural Power of a Transformed Mind* by Bill Johnson. We loved discussing the rich lessons contained in his writing, and in the chapter on "Enduring Uncertainty," there is an excerpt about the lies of the enemy that is deeply convicting:

> Christians want answers so badly during times of un-
> certainty that they invent theological answers to make
> themselves feel good about their present condition.
> In doing so, they sacrifice the truth about God on the
> altar of human reasoning. That's what causes people to
> say things like, "God gave my aunt leukemia to teach
> her perseverance." No way. That has never happened.

If somebody's body is racked with pain or wasting away because of disease, it's the devourer. It's not the job description of the Messiah. Again, the Bible says, "He forgives all your iniquities; He heals all your diseases." It would never enter our minds that God would give someone a drug habit or a drinking problem to help them become better people. So why would He condemn people to disease? Or poverty? Or depression? Or any other miserable condition? Let's get this straight: God is good all of the time. The devil is bad all of the time. We do ourselves a tremendous service to remember the difference between the two. Healing, salvation, wholeness, provision, and joy have already been given to us. They can't be recalled or returned. They are facts of Kingdom living. They were paid for by Jesus on the Cross.

Other Christians fall into the deception that when the Bible talks about sufferings, it means all of the above afflictions. Not at all! The suffering referred to in the Bible means living between two conflicting realities and trusting and praising God through it all. Anybody can declare the greatness of God after they've won the Reader's Digest sweepstakes. But when you live in the middle of a conflict—of having a promise that is not yet fulfilled, or having a problem that seems to never get resolved—you rise above circumstance and declare that He is good all the time, no matter what.[8]

Biblical suffering: "living between two conflicting realities and trusting and praising God through it all." That rings with truth. And God is good. All of the time. No matter what.

Heavenly Father, you are good all of the time and we praise you for your faithfulness to us in every circumstance. The enemy came to steal, kill, and destroy, but Jesus came to heal, fill, and restore. Thank you that you are the good Shepherd who gave your life that we might live, and that you cradle us in arms that will never let us go. We pray this in the name of Jesus, Amen.

Do nothing out of selfish ambition or vain conceit. Rather, in humility value others above yourselves, not looking to your own interests but each of you to the interests of the others. —Philippians 2:3-4

13

Humility

At Carrie's memorial service on Friday, July 6, 2007, I shared with the congregation what she had told me several months earlier: "I asked the Lord to humble me, and boy, is He ever answering that request!" It was so evident in Carrie's life that her first desire was to serve her Savior and Lord, and she did not want any element in her life to detract from that goal. She never spent a great deal of time bemoaning the assault the cancer had waged on her body; she bore it with consummate dignity, believing the truth in Paul's words from 2 Corinthians 4:16-18:

> Therefore we do not lose heart. Though outwardly we are wasting away, yet inwardly we are being renewed day by day. For our light and momentary troubles are achieving for us an eternal glory that far outweighs them all. So we fix our eyes not on what is seen, but on what is unseen. For what is seen is temporary, but what is unseen is eternal.

There is a great difference between genuine humility and false modesty. We may graciously demur when praised for our attributes or performance, but this is not really humility. The essence of being humble is the willingness to be placed in any aspect of service to God; the willingness to lose ourselves for His sake, regardless of the cost to ourselves. It is epitomized by the passage in Philippians 2:5-8:

> Your attitude should be the same as that of Christ Jesus; Who, being in very nature God, did not consider equality with God something to be grasped, but made Himself nothing, taking the very nature of a servant, being made in human likeness. And being found in appearance as a man, He humbled Himself and became obedient to death—even death on a cross!

The Lord has had a sizable job in driving that truth home for me. I don't think that I probably appeared vain or conceited to most—I certainly hope not! But there was definitely a heart change that needed to take place in me. Having been given the gift of music, I learned early on that there was much acclaim to be garnered from family, friends, and even strangers when I played the piano. Along with that, I became overly concerned with my physical appearance, as they seemed to go hand in hand when one was in the public eye. Although I was careful to receive compliments with modesty, my vain "evil twin" (as Carrie liked to call it) was sopping them up with glee. I made a point of sharing my talent in church, nursing homes, and other charitable venues, but the glory was not for God; it went right to me.

My day of reckoning came in December of 1983. I had been visiting my parents in Chicago and returned to Denver in the midst of an Arctic blast that burst the pipes in my house. Water was flooding the first floor, and in an effort to save my possessions, I severely injured the tendons in my right wrist. I was told by several different specialists that the damage was permanent and that I would probably never again play the piano the way I once had. For someone whose identity was wrapped up in her profession, this was devastating news. I had no choice but to continue to play, as that was my livelihood, but I was in constant, unrelenting pain.

Despite painkillers, braces, and balms, I could find no relief. In utter desperation, I sensed the Lord trying to tell me something: "You shall have no other gods before Me." Me, an idolater? Yes, that was exactly what I was.

I had agreed to play a Bach concerto on the harpsichord at my church, Cherry Creek Presbyterian, on the first Sunday in December of 1985. Having struggled with this pain for two years, I had simply resigned myself to it and did the best I could under the circumstances. But driving home from the Saturday rehearsal, I felt a sensation so intense that I didn't know whether I could endure it, as if my arm were being consumed in flames. I cried out, "Lord, if you want me to do this, then I give it to you for your glory and not for mine! And if you don't want me to do this anymore, show me something else to do!" Nothing changed physically, but I began to sense His peace come over me.

The next morning, I played the two services at church and didn't think anything of it until one of the pastors came up to me and asked about my arm. Suddenly I realized that there was absolutely NO PAIN! The absence of it was startling. I thanked God for this reprieve, thinking that He was blessing me for yielding this to Him. Little did I know that He had just, by His own hand, completely healed my affliction. From that moment, I kept my promise to give Him the glory in my music.

As time went on, God revealed other areas in my life that needed a similar yielding in order that I might be conformed to the image of Christ. On October 14, 2000, Philippe and I were rollerblading a few miles from our home when I suddenly tripped over a hose at a construction site. Rushed to the hospital by ambulance, I had no idea what the ramifications of this injury would be over time. The most obvious was a hole above my upper lip and a broken front tooth; these were readily repaired. The most serious was an injury to two cervical vertebrae in my neck.

Once again, I was faced with unremitting and often excruciating pain, to the extent that there were nights I could not even lie down. I would walk up and down our stairs most of the night, crying out to the Lord. An MRI of my brain indicated what appeared to be a potentially lethal twisting of the left vertebral artery, and I was told to curtail my physical activities pending diagnostic brain surgery.

The fear that entered my being was different from that which I had experienced with my cancer diagnosis. This time, I was told that the surgery carried with it the risk of a stroke during the procedure. I began to imagine what on earth I'd do if I were left paralyzed, unable to feed or groom myself, unable to talk or sing —and certainly not able to play the piano! I was allowing my imagination to take me to places I didn't need to go.

My surgery was scheduled for Maundy Thursday in April of 2001. I was listening to Chuck Swindoll on the radio in my car on Tuesday of that week, and he was delivering a message on Calvary. As I pulled into the Target parking lot, he was preaching about being willing to bring all we are to the cross, and I suddenly GOT it! This wasn't about me at all; this was about HIM! I was at my own personal Calvary, facing the unknown with desperate fear. But He, my Lord Jesus Christ, had gone before me and paid it all, so I could face what I had to face knowing that all I had to do was put my trust in Him. Nothing would happen to me that He would not permit, and everything that did happen, He would work together for good. An enormous burden lifted that day, and this was another giant step forward in my understanding of true humility. I knew that even if I experienced what I dreaded most, God was still God and I would praise Him in whatever circumstances I found myself. Even if I were incapacitated, I would give Him glory.

Blessedly, everything went beautifully and what had appeared to be a twisted artery was actually a congenital anomaly: I was born without it—a much better scenario! The Lord had allowed me to walk through this life lesson because He knew I needed it, and He was glorified through it. He taught me that I didn't need to DO anything; I simply had to be yielded as His vessel and willing to be used in whatever fashion He deemed necessary. It all comes back to the Cross, as the words of Isaac Watts remind us:

> When I survey the wondrous cross
> On which the Prince of glory died,
> My richest gain I count but loss,
> And pour contempt on all my pride.
>
> Forbid it, Lord, that I should boast,
> Save in the death of Christ, my God;
> All the vain things that charm me most-
> I sacrifice them to his blood.

An attitude of humility is the only way in which we can truly worship God in spirit and in truth. We have to de-throne ourselves and bow before the King of kings and the Lord of lords, allowing Him access to remodel our bodies, minds and spirits. "For everyone who exalts himself will be humbled, and he who humbles himself will be exalted" (Luke 14:11).

Gracious and loving God, we thank you for Jesus, who humbled Himself to death, even death on a cross. You have made us in your image, and are conforming us to the likeness of Christ. Grant us the willingness to yield to your Lordship, working out our salvation with fear and trembling, knowing that it is you who are working in us to will and to act according to your good purpose. We give you all the glory, in Jesus' name. Amen.

Friends come and friends go, but a true friend sticks by you like family.
—*Proverbs 18:24 (MSG)*

14

Grown-up Girlfriends

When I first met Carrie, she was still in the process of collaborating with her dear friend Erin Smalley on their book, *Grown-Up Girlfriends*. I was privileged to hear snippets here and there of how it was all progressing, and delighted when Carrie presented me with my own autographed copy. Imagine my amazement when I learned that my precious cousin Maggie, who had just been hired by Tyndale as a publicist in the spring of 2007, informed me that she had been assigned to help work on this book! It was one of those "divine coincidences" that made me smile with infinite joy and wonder at the intricacy of God's hand. He was linking two of my most special friends together!

This wasn't the first time that God had orchestrated one of these amazing bridges in my friendships. It was through our mutual close friend Barb Tallant that I heard of Carrie in the first place, and was praying for her long before I ever knew I would meet her. God had designed this amazing tapestry and prepared in advance these things that we would do together.

Carrie writes about this in the second chapter of *Grown-Up Girlfriends*:

If we truly recognize that the Lord is in control of whom we cross paths with, it becomes easier to see that our relationships are really about HIM and not US! We have to admit that when we enter into a new relationship, we often do so because it feels good or it meets a need for us. We feel loved, valued, and worthwhile. The relationship may fill gaps in our lives. Will we continue in a friendship simply because it meets our needs, or are we willing to truly seek how the Lord might be leading us to higher ground or using us to encourage our friend to higher places?[9]

As I wrote in the opening pages of this book, our pastor Stew Grant had asked me to come alongside Carrie and befriend her during the times she would come to Houston for treatment at M.D. Anderson. From our very first telephone conversation, however, I knew that this would be more than a temporary assignment! God was blessing me with a grown-up girlfriend who would add immeasurably to my life. There was an instant bond that transcended the normal boundaries of new friendship: we were soldiers in the battle against cancer, but even more, we were soldiers of the Cross. This made for a powerful sisterhood!

Carrie writes about this in chapter eleven of *Grown-Up Girl-friends:*

Pancreatic cancer has a 4 percent survival rate. I did not know this in the beginning because I refused to look at any Web sites on this stinky cancer. I refused to be a statistic, but I saw the concern in people's eyes and knew I had a long, tough battle to fight.

Several weeks ago I heard a message at church on how we learn endurance while going through trials. The apostle James began his letter by reminding us that when our endurance is tested we have a chance to grow so that we can be strong in character. "Consider it pure joy," he said, "whenever you face trials of many kinds, because you know that the testing of your faith develops perseverance. Perseverance must finish its work so that you may be mature and complete, not lacking anything" (James 1:2-4).

There it is again, the idea of growing and maturing. Grown-up girlfriends have the opportunity to grow with someone in her trial and to bring joy in the midst of grief, pain, doubt, and anger. Often a suffering person is not thinking about growing or enduring. Instead she is thinking, "Why, God?" or "How will I make it through?" or "Is anybody really there for me?" As James points out, crisis can be an opportunity to learn new and better ways of coping. However, it can also be lethal if we stay in despair and fall into depression, alienation, and hopelessness. Sometimes having a grown-up girlfriend to walk with through the crisis can make all the difference.[10]

One of the most life-changing aspects of my friendship with Carrie came from observing how she had learned to allow friends to walk through crisis with her. My own tendency as an independent, contemplative, artistic and often introverted individual had been to try to manage on my own, looking to God and to my husband, but generally not outward to include others. I saw how easily she appeared to be able to ask for help, not making apologies for "inconveniencing" anyone as I would usually do, but more from the standpoint of "this is what friends do for one another." It was also never, ever one-sided. She was lavish in her prayer support, conversational topics, card and e-mail correspondence, and gift-giving. However, I didn't realize that she had worked on these skills until I read what she had written in *Grown-Up Girlfriends!*

I have discovered some valuable insights into myself through my own crisis. To admit aloud that I need anything is difficult for me. My fear is that nobody will sign up to help with those needs, so I won't ask, thereby avoiding the rejection. I'm sure this comes from all sorts of roots—growing up as the independent middle child in a family that didn't often signal our needs to each other, as well as being rejected by a friend and not wanting to risk that feeling again. Yet the bottom line is that I am still responsible to function as God asks me to in the midst of crisis. I am to face it, name it, need in it, and learn from it."[11]

I was truly honored when Carrie would ask me to do something for her. I remember her calling me to say that she would be needing a minor surgical procedure on her stent and that she had to be at M.D. Anderson by 5:30 a.m. This meant that I would need to get up at 3:15 in order to leave at 4 and pick her up at the Hanna's at 5. As I pulled up to the curb in the pitch-dark, I saw the frail form of the waiflike Carrie moving tenuously towards my car. I just wanted to hightail it to Starbucks with her and ditch the idea of the hospital! However, we dutifully proceeded with the plan and ended up ultimately having a delightful time together. We would always somehow make light of whatever the situation held, knowing that our heavenly Father held us.

One day in early April of 2007, Carrie phoned me to discuss the e-mail she had sent in which she suggested we collaborate on a book. "I really think we're supposed to write a book together on walking through cancer as Christians." My heart was leaping for joy, as I had felt the Lord impressing on me for years the call to recount in writing my testimony about cancer and my other life trials, never anticipating that I would share in the endeavor with a friend. We excitedly made tentative plans for me to go to Siloam Springs in mid-May for a preliminary planning retreat, but I was amused when I got an e-mail from her the day before Easter with a disclaimer or two:

CARRIE

Why you might have second thoughts about writing with me? I am procrastinat-

ing like the dickens. I need to be doing a re-write on a chapter right now [on a book with Gary], but as you can see, I am emailing, cooking, doing other things instead. I really should get this done before I leave tomorrow. I just keep putting it off; did all week! Got many other things done! Well, I know it will get finished. I actually need a little break from writing, but I know without any shadow of a doubt that this cancer book is supposed to be written, and I do believe by us both. I can't wait to see God make it happen!

With the death of Matt Oliver on May 6, 2007 and Carrie's subsequent rapid decline, we were never able to even outline this book together, but God kept His promise and provided a way through Gary's permission for me to use her online journal as the basis for her part of this book. It is pure joy for me to spend time with such vibrant memories of Carrie as the Lord leads me in this; her friendship remains so vital a part of who I am.

Over the relatively brief course of our intense friendship, Carrie gave me many gifts, one of which was a little book called *A Girlfriend is a Sister You Choose*. One of the entries reads:

Girlfriends always carry each other in their hearts. Whether they live near each other or far apart, girlfriends walk through life together. They're there for each other no matter what, sharing everything…Girlfriends are connected at the heart, and their loyalty to one another is permanent. No one can ever break that bond. They don't give up on each other easily. They have the utmost sensitivity and compassion for one another. Girlfriends aren't afraid to break rules for each other. They defend each other; they take chances for each other. They've cried together and laughed together. They know each other's secrets, and they can almost read each other's mind…Girlfriends teach each other lessons as they stand by each other in life, and they are there for each other through everything that matters. No one can ever take the place of a girlfriend.

Thank you for being mine. I carry you in my heart forever and always.[12]

In many ways because of my friendship with Carrie, I have been able to embrace friendships with other women as never before. I have become much more receptive to allowing them to minister to me rather than in needing to always be the caregiver. Even in the immediate aftermath of Carrie's death, my other friends gathered around, phoned or wrote to comfort me and I thought of how selfless they were to minister to me in this way and to not be threatened by my deep expressions of loss. I realized that there is no possessiveness in true friendship, or the need to be Number One. Each friend is unique and irreplaceable, having an indelible impact on our lives.

My cousin Maggie, the grown-up girlfriend I've known and loved the longest (next to my mom, naturally), called me one day last fall and suggested a Sisters' Weekend with her older sister Cindy, sister-in-law Jody, and myself (who snuck into that category because Maggie and I call each other CSF, which stands for "Cousin, Sister, Friend"). This is something I probably would never have done before knowing Carrie, but she taught me the value of spending time with the people we love and of cherishing every moment together. So, the four of us "sisters" gathered at the Charleston, SC airport at around midnight on March 19, 2009, and spent two and a half days visiting plantations, shopping at the downtown market and buying souvenirs, strolling along the waterway, devouring scrumptious Southern home cooking, laughing and crying and then laughing some more. We're already looking forward to the next one!

Carrie had many, many grown-up girlfriends, most of whom I never even saw until her memorial service. However, I felt as though I knew them, too, as she would speak of them and write to me about them and include them in her journal entries and in her book. She loved them all deeply and saw them as part of God's provision and plan for her life. Each relationship was unique in its dynamics and essential to her life. Every friendship helped to build her into the godly woman that she had become.

Carrie also had a few girlfriends who were not quite grown-up yet. And a notable one was Gigi Hanna, the seven-year-old daughter of the Oliver's dear friends Sylvie and Ehab Hanna. With the wisdom of a child, Gigi wrote a poem that Carrie included in *Grown-Up Girlfriends* in her chapter on "Why God Calls Us to Grown-Up Friendships." I'm particularly partial to it because Carrie had taken to calling me "Twin" as the similarities in our personalities became more and more evident with time. I think that Gigi understands what it's all about:

How to be a Friend

Be nice and kind.
Play with them.
Let them win.
Give them a nickel.
Send them e-mails.
When they are sick, make them a card.
Ask them for a playdate.
Say great things about them.
Say it's awesome to be twins.[13]

Carrie, it was awesome to be your "twin"! I am so grateful for the gift of your friendship and the knowledge that we will one day be sisters again in heaven!

Precious Lord, we give you thanks for all good things and especially today for the gift of friendships that are anchored in Christ. We are so grateful that these transcend time and place because you have promised us that where you are, we will be also. Help us to always strive to love one another as you have first loved us. In Jesus' name, Amen.

Whether you turn to the right or to the left, your ears will hear a voice behind you, saying, "This is the way; walk in it." —Isaiah 30:21

15

The Journey

In late May of 2007, my husband, our son Paul and I took a trip to Africa. This entailed a flight from Houston to Amsterdam, a one-night layover in The Netherlands, and a ten-hour flight the next day to Johannesburg, South Africa. We then rented a car and drove for a while, spending the night at a quaint inn, before continuing on the next day to the Kruger National Park. Our bodies, especially our cramped legs, told us that this was a journey! However, we were rewarded with a veritable Garden of Eden: an array of God's Creation nearly indescribable in its beauty and variety. Around nearly every bend in the road, we would be greeted by a work of His hand: a family of five warthogs ambling down a sunny path; a cluster of cheetah cubs nestled in a little gulley; dizzying zebras by the dozen; a cacophonous family of monkeys scavenging for tourist leftovers. The time spent getting there was forgotten in light of the rewards awaiting us.

I started thinking about what constitutes a "journey." The word certainly connotes much more than a trip, and in fact, it may not imply travel at all. What a journey does signify is a matter of endurance through change. Cancer is definitely a journey.

CARRIE

Journal entry, December 4, 2006: It's a "journey," this life we are walking and living. Do you think of your life as a journey? Since the diagnosis, I have had several prayer warriors say to me that they truly believe that I would experience healing, but that I would walk a "journey" before that would take place. I have been thinking about the experience of "journey" as time continues to pass, and I keep walking.

To journey means to pass from one place to another. I like the word "journey" and am interested in thinking more about the meaning. When I think of "journey" and the passing from one place to another, I think of the experiences, the people and relationships involved in the process. Each and every one of us are moving: from one experience to another, from one season to another, from the finite life we lead on earth to an eternal life after we die.

Carrie's perception of a journey is one that involved many physical changes, but far more than that, myriad spiritual changes. My own journey through cancer took some unique twists and turns, but always with the knowledge that the Lord was preparing and leading the way, even if my feelings lagged a few spiritual miles behind! When Carrie described the day of her pancreatic cancer diagnosis as an "out-of-body" experience, I could fully relate to that sensation. A "trip" to the doctor's office became the journey of a lifetime.

For me, it seemed like I was little Lucy emerging from the wardrobe into the strange land of Narnia in C.S. Lewis' *The Lion, the Witch, and the Wardrobe*. Walking through the door of an ordinary medical office took me into a whole new and terrifying world where everything seemed foreign and hostile. I hadn't "journeyed" further than a few miles down the road, but my whole life was instantly changed. Over time, though, I became aware of the fact that the Lion of Judah, my Lord and Savior Jesus Christ, was always at my side. He provided a loving and encouraging husband, parents, and extended family to come alongside me through this journey. He supplied doctors and nurses to be His anointed hands of healing. He encouraged me through the body of Christ, His church. He abided with me through one abdominal surgery after another, comforting me by the power of the Holy Spirit whispering words of healing love. He was, and is, always on this journey with me.

CARRIE

Journal entry, February 19, 2006: Just finished reading the book A Bend in the Road *by Dr. David Jeremiah and really enjoyed hearing his story of walking through cancer. The book offers great spiritual wisdom and insight into who God is in the midst of crisis and how he changes us as we walk the crisis journey. As I finished this book, I did some thinking about "bends in our road." Does our road we walk come with twists and turns? Are there bends? Does it really matter how we look at this? I decided it does, for these reasons: Scripture talks about walking the "straight" path; that he will make our paths straight and that we are not to look to the left or right, leaning on our own understanding. Cancer has not been a bend in my path. That is to say that the bends, the twists, are where I go when I choose to listen to fear, to depression, to hopelessness, to temptation, to giving up, to what the world offers, etc.*

God is very capable of keeping us straight, but we have to "show up" from our ventures to the left and right or from the dark forest we have run into for a while, convinced it will bring us pleasure and numb our pain. I find great comfort in knowing that God has straight paths for us and that when the things come into our lives that threaten to knock us off this path or distract us from it, He will be there to gently guide us back. All we have to do is turn our eyes to His face and look straight ahead to meet His eyes. In walking that path, there is peace and calm and perfect alignment; no twists and turns, just two walking together in union.

Carrie found that the only way take a journey is with Jesus. Turning our eyes upon Jesus, just like the old hymn says, and looking full into His wonderful face, the things of earth do grow strangely dim in the light of His glory and grace. Remembering that we were created in the image of God to know and enjoy Him forever; that He has plans to prosper our lives and to give us hope and a future; that He loves us with an everlasting love and holds us in His everlasting arms; that He will never leave us or forsake us: these are His promises, and He who promised is faithful!

Like any journey, there is an element of comfort that comes with familiarity. The "firsts" always seem to be the hardest: the first CT scan; the first chemo, radiation, or hormonal treatment; the first MRI; the first surgery. We dread the unknown. Then we see that Jesus Christ, who is the same yesterday, today and forever (Hebrews 13:8), has been with us all along, loving and abiding with us. We just have to let go of the fear long enough to see Him. Then the journey becomes a walk of faith.

My journey has involved five abdominal surgeries, diagnostic brain surgery, spinal surgery and a diagnosis of premature osteopenia due to estrogen deprivation from the complete hysterectomy at a young age. At first, I felt that my body had betrayed me; that it was unpredictable and even hostile. I didn't like it at all! Then I began to see that my physical being was indeed the temple of God's Holy Spirit: His dwelling place in me while I am on this earth. This body will eventually wither and fade like the flowers and the grass, but the Spirit of Christ in me, the hope of glory, will endure forever. Knowing that one day I will have a new and perfect body that will never be sick gives me hope to run with perseverance the race that is still before me.

CARRIE

Journal entry, September 15, 2005: I feel I am in one of those long-distance races right now in my journey. For those of you who run, you know it's the place where it is hard to keep going—but what are your choices? Run off to the side? NO. Stop? NO. Start walking? NO. These are not options. The place in the mile that happens is about 1.5 to 2 laps, knowing there are 2 full laps to go. Really, I don't know how many laps I have yet to go. I could be in a marathon. I just know it feels like that place where it gets hard. I have cheerleaders, though; people standing on the sidelines—and they keep me going. Truth keeps me going in the race and sustains me when I look at the laps I have remaining to run.

It helps me to think of the saints of the ages who have run with perseverance the race —the journey—set before them. They have endured strife and peril, sword and persecution; they have been censored and beaten senseless; they have been fired at and burned in the fires. They have upheld the name of the Lord Jesus Christ to the end of their earthly existence, knowing that they were not living for this world, but for the Life that will never end. They have fought the good fight, finished the course, and kept the faith.

John Bunyan alludes to this in the preface, which he calls "The Author's Apology," to his classic allegory *The Pilgrim's Progress*:

> And now, before I do put up my pen,
> I'll show the profit of my book, and then
> Commit both thee and it unto that Hand
> That pulls the strong down, and makes weak
> ones stand.
>
> This book it chalketh out before thine eyes
> The man who seeks the everlasting prize.
> It shows you whence he came, whither he goes;
> What he leaves undone, also what he does;
> It shows you how he runs and runs
> Till he unto the gate of glory comes.
>
> It shows, too, who set out for life a main,
> As if the lasting crown they would obtain;
> Here also you may see the reason why
> They lose their labor, and like fools do die.

This book will make a traveler of thee,
If by its counsels thou wilt ruled be;
It will direct thee to the Holy Land,
If thou wilt its directions understand:
Yea, it will make the slothful active be;
The blind also delightful things to see.

Wouldst thou read thyself? Oh, then come hither,
And lay my book, thy head and heart together.[14]

The apostle Peter, who was martyred for his faith in Christ, sums it all up in the words that he was inspired to write in I Peter 1:3-9:

Praise be to the God and Father of our Lord Jesus Christ! In His great mercy He has given us new birth into a living hope through the resurrection of Jesus Christ from the dead, and into an inheritance that can never perish, spoil or fade—kept in heaven for you, who through faith are shielded by God's power until the coming of the salvation that is ready to be revealed in the last time. In this you will greatly rejoice, though now for a little while you may have had to suffer grief in all kinds of trials. These have come so that your faith—of greater worth than gold, which perishes even though refined by fire—may be proved genuine and may result in praise, glory and honor when Jesus Christ is revealed. Though you have not seen Him, you love Him; and even though you do not see Him now, you believe in Him and are filled with an inexpressible and glorious joy, for you are receiving the goal of your faith, the salvation of your souls.

Jesus IS the journey!

Precious Lord, You have not left us alone in this journey of life, but you walk beside us and you carry us when the burden is too heavy to bear. Thank you for your Truth that inspires us, your strength that sustains us, and your love that lifts us above the things of this earth. We pray in Jesus' name, Amen.

For He will command His angels concerning you to guard you in all your ways; they will lift you up in their hands, so that you will not strike your foot against a stone. —Psalm 91:11-12

16

Angels

My foot hit the brake without my even being consciously aware of it, and the vehicle behind us blared its horn. Our sixteen-year-old son Paul admonished, "Mom, you don't brake for a green light!"—and then we saw the car careening around the corner in an illegal left turn. The sequence of events happened in a split second, but after I caught my breath, I said to Paul, "Angels put those brakes on for me."

This happened just two nights ago, and is only one of countless incidences of the angels of the Lord encamping around us, lifting us up in their hands at the bidding of our heavenly Father to protect us from the dangers in the world. I suspect that most of the time, we are not aware of them and simply think we escaped by the skin of our teeth or, in the eyes of the secular world, "got lucky." But angels are part of God's creation and Kingdom design.

Stories of the angelic host abound in the Bible, both in the Old and New Testament. The first reference is in Genesis 16, where an angel of the Lord appears to Hagar, the maidservant of Abram's wife Sarai, to tell her to return to her mistress and submit to her. The angel tells Hagar that she is with child, and that she is to name him Ishmael. He goes on to describe what the child will be like (and I personally would not have taken that as good news): that he will be like a wild donkey and live in hostility toward all his brothers. However, Hagar responds to the message from the Lord by saying, "You are the God who sees me" (Genesis 16:13).

Angels were created by God to be His messengers. Most Christians are probably familiar with the account of the angel visiting Joseph in a dream to say, "Joseph son of David, do not be afraid to take Mary home to be your wife, because what is conceived in her is from the Holy Spirit. She will give birth to a son, and you are to give him the name Jesus, because he will save his people from their sins" (Matthew 1:20). An angel of the Lord appeared again to Joseph after the birth of Jesus to warn him to take his family to Egypt to escape King Herod, and later on to tell them to return to Israel after Herod's death. Joseph faithfully followed these instructions.

Perhaps the most familiar reference to angels is from Luke 2:10-14, where an angel of the Lord appeared to shepherds in the fields outside of Bethlehem one night:

> "Do not be afraid. I bring you good news that will cause great joy for all the people. Today in the town of David a Savior has been born to you; he is the Messiah, the Lord. This will be a sign to you: You will find a baby wrapped in cloths and lying in a manger." Suddenly a great company of the heavenly host appeared with the angel, praising God and saying, "Glory to God in the highest heaven, and on earth peace to those on whom his favor rests."

The gospels of Matthew, Mark and Luke all record the appearance of an angel (or in the case of Luke, two angels) at the entrance to the empty tomb after the crucifixion of Jesus. The description of the angel in Matthew 28:3 reads, "His appearance was like lightning, and his clothes were white as snow." The common human reaction to the appearance of an angel seems to be fear, for they are often reported to have said, "Fear not" or "Do not be afraid." The majesty and brilliance of the angels of the Lord are breathtaking.

I'm not much of a television watcher, but I must say that the series *Touched by an Angel* was a favorite! Especially after my cancer experience and the brushes with death that followed, I became more and more aware of the knowledge of God's supernatural provision for our well-being, using His heavenly messengers. I have heard many accounts of angel sightings, and have actually experienced one myself.

It was late in May of 2007, and we were preparing to leave for Africa. Philippe, Paul and I had felt a call from God to go to Uganda to visit Stephen, one of the children that we sponsor through Compassion International. This was an enormous step of faith, requiring intricate planning, visas, and multiple inoculations. Because of my rather precarious health history, and knowing that we would be in very primitive conditions for several days, I must admit that I was anxious. Two nights before we were to depart from Houston, I was alone in our bedroom (Philippe was flying), tossing and turning in bed. Suddenly I was aware of a brilliant white light by the side of the bed, and a feeling of profound peace enveloped me. I did not see any specific features, but was aware that this was an angelic messenger from God to remind me that "He will command His angels concerning you to guard you in all your ways" (Psalm 91:11). It was a special gift from God to reassure me of His protection over us as we ventured out in faith.

Although it is hard to "prove" that one has seen an angel, it comforts me greatly to be aware that God takes care of us in this way. The book of Hebrews, in chapter 13, verse 2, exhorts us: "Do not forget to entertain strangers, for by so doing some people have entertained angels without knowing it." I sometimes wonder about those who perform extraordinary acts of kindness or mercy for others, and wonder if they are really angels. I think that our loving God probably disguises His angels in many everyday situations without our ever being aware of who they really are. I wouldn't be surprised to find out that there are gardeners, custodians, waitresses, gas station attendants, Wal-Mart associates, tollbooth agents—you name it—doing the Lord's work in this way. I'm certain that many of them regularly inhabit hospitals.

It was the Friday before Christmas in the year 2001, and we were in Denver to be with my parents as my dad had exploratory surgery at University Hospital. Early in the evening, we learned from one of the attending physicians that Dad had inoperable metastatic cancer of the prostate. I was with Mom, and we were in the throes of shock and grief. We went up to the floor where Dad's room was, and when they wheeled him in on the gurney, I tried in vain to withhold my tears as I rubbed his sweet bald head. Suddenly, a woman emerged from a room behind me, embraced me with such warmth that it was truly the touch of God, and said, "God cannot do one thing: He cannot lie." She uttered a few more words of comfort, and disappeared. I never saw her again, but she was a messenger from God, angelic or not. She's probably what I refer to as an "earth angel."

CARRIE

Journal entry, August 15, 2006: Today a miracle happened. An angel came to me. Truthfully, this was a "real" person, but she was an angel to me. Gary, Andrew and I have been here at The Plaza in Kansas City since we arrived yesterday. We were sitting at "Latte Land" outdoors around 7:30 p.m. enjoying coffee, the people, reading and chatting when a dear woman came around to my side of the rail and leaned down and said, "Carrie?" I said, "Yes?" She said, "I am Kim and you came to my dorm room on the day of the Delta Gamma selection of my freshman year at UNL to give me my invitation to become a DG, and I have been reading your website faithfully and have been praying for you." I, of course, started crying as she said hello to Andrew, calling him by name, and to Gary, knowing them from the website, and asked Andrew how his Ireland trip had gone. She was a block and a half down the street when she turned to her family and said, "I really think that was Carrie Oliver back there." She was here from Nebraska. Her 17-year-old daughter said, "Mom, you need to go back and see," so she did—and she was my angel. She blessed me with her smile, her encouragement, her energy, and her belief that I was going to live. She said, "You will be that 4%, Carrie."

Why was this woman my angel on this Saturday in August of 2006? The last two weeks could be summed up as probably the most difficult I have experienced since this disease. I have struggled with some serious spiritual warfare. The enemy has thrown it all out there. Through relationships, through my health, and that dang fear that I have struggled with all of my life. It crept back in this past week. I have been so faithful in overcoming fear, but like most humans—and yes, it's true, I am a weak little human being—I have failed in the fear area lately.

The hard thing about fear is that no person can make it better for you. Only you can get it under control, and that means a lot of going to the Word and truth of God and going to God Himself. I have been talking to Him a great deal. The very wonderful news is that He is faithful, and this morning I was feeling much less fearful. The scriptures that I go to often are, "Do not lean on your own understanding (Proverbs 3:5); "Cast all your anxiety on Him" (Philippians 4:6); "Do not be afraid of the dangers by day or the terrors at night" (Psalm 91:5-6), and so many more. The Word is my friend when the strength of others cannot supply. I am constantly in this learning process and know that peace on earth is one hard thing to accomplish, but is oh, so sweet when experienced.

I, like my dear friend Carrie, have experienced the boundless provision of God through all circumstances and every emotion. I have seen proof more times than I can enumerate that "My God will meet all your needs according to His glorious riches in Christ Jesus" (Philippians 4:19). God anticipates our needs as He promises in Isaiah 65:24, "Before they call, I will answer; while they are still speaking, I will hear." And He does command His angels to guard us in all our ways. Heavenly angels—and earth angels. Thanks be to God!

Dear Lord, it is with awe that we regard your provision for all of our needs. You have given us a Savior, Jesus Christ; a Counselor, the Holy Spirit; and you have created an angelic host to watch over us in all of our ways. We stand before you with humble adoration and great thanksgiving, praying this in Jesus' name, Amen.

He gives strength to the weary and increases the power of the weak. Even youths grow tired and weary, and young men stumble and fall; but those who hope in the Lord will renew their strength. They will soar on wings like eagles; they will run and not grow weary; they will walk and not be faint.
—Isaiah 40:29-31

17

Waiting

Well, another billowing roll of the waves of life nearly knocked the breath out of us yesterday. I had taken our sixteen-year-old son Paul to the endocrinologist to learn the results of his fasting glucose and lipids tests. We had been told two months earlier, in April of 2008, that Paul had insulin resistance, and that it was imperative for him to lose weight quickly and establish a daily exercise program. To his credit, he persevered and lost twenty-one pounds, which greatly improved his body chemistry over eight weeks. We anticipated only good news yesterday.

Paul's doctor showed concern on his face as he went through the reports. He told us that he wanted to do another test as soon as possible because he suspected Paul had excessive growth hormone, which has as its source a tumor in the pituitary gland in the brain. The very mention of that word, "tumor," set us reeling. Been there, done that—enough! When the doctor left to make arrangements for the test, Paul and I sat there like we'd been slam-dunked by that wave.

Paul's first reaction was one of anger. He had just put forth colossal effort to completely alter his eating habits and to work out every day in order to lose weight to prevent diabetes, and he's told that he might have a brain tumor! Life is just not fair! Having lived through a similar scenario myself, I knew enough to not stuff scripture down his throat, but to wait...to wait on the Lord. To trust in Him, and lean not unto my own understanding. To abide in Him and wait for His voice.

Tears came to my eyes, which is a pretty typical reaction for me. This seemed to upset Paul further, but perhaps he really needed to see how much I cared. I looked over at him and whispered, "Sweetheart, if I could take that test for you, I would...but I can't. If I could take that tumor from you, if there even is one, I would, but I can't. But Dad and I will do everything we can to help you through this." At that moment, Paul was angry at God, but he needed to know that his parents would be there for him. I was acting as God's representative to one who felt so distant from Him. I only knew to do that because others had done it for me.

After my cancer diagnosis in 1990, the Lord gave me the gift of a "life verse" which He had written on my heart, Psalm 27:13-14, "I am still confident of this: I will see the goodness of the Lord in the land of the living. Wait for the Lord; be strong and take heart and wait for the Lord." Because I have seen the fulfillment of this promise over and over throughout the past nearly two decades, I have the proof of this truth, and it has become my testimony.

Paul is still very much in the process of discovering God's faithfulness for himself, and neither Philippe nor I can expedite the process except by being living examples of the work of Christ in our own lives. One of the phrases I think of so often when I am in a situation where God is growing the faith of someone I love is from Oswald Chambers in the classic devotional, *My Utmost for His Highest.* He says in the entry for August 1:

> Are we playing the spiritual amateur providence in other lives? Are we so noisy in our instruction of others that God cannot get anywhere near them? We have to keep our mouths shut and our spirits alert.

God wants to instruct us in regard to His Son, He wants to turn our times of prayer into mounts of transfiguration, and we will not let Him. When we are certain of the way God is going to work, He will never work in that way anymore. He works where He sends us to wait. Wait on God and He will work, but don't wait in spiritual sulks because you cannot see an inch in front of you! Are we detached enough from our own spiritual hysterics to wait on God? To wait is not to sit with folded hands, but to learn to do what we are told.[15]

Our job as parents of Paul de Chambrier is to love him and instruct him in the ways of the Lord. We are to set a holy example for him, and to rejoice with him in psalms and hymns and spiritual songs. We are to help him to hide God's word in his heart, and to seek Him day and night. We are to pray with him and for him. After that, we must wait. We must trust that God is leading this young man down his own unique path, and that His plan is to prosper Paul and not to harm him; to give him hope and a future. We must allow Paul to arm-wrestle with God if necessary, so that he can develop his own spiritual muscles of faith. It's not easy to step back when your child is in pain. The bottom line is that Paul is God's beloved son first, and our Father knows best.

Philippe and I have learned through the timeless School of Hard Knocks that the Lord answers before we call, even if we do not hear Him at first. I dropped Paul off at his friend's house after that appointment, where he had been invited to have dinner and spend the night. Returning to our home, I poured out the details to Philippe, and even as we scrounged around to assemble a hasty meal, we began praising God and affirming His character and promises. Later in the evening, I felt a prompting to share with the mom of Paul's friend Jordan about what we had learned that day. To my amazement, Paul had openly revealed all of this to her and she had begun reassuring and encouraging him. Her husband, a physician, joined in with some very helpful advice, and I knew that the Lord had put His plan in motion before we even knew what was happening. The beauty is that Paul felt the hand of God on this situation and that these friends were also edified by their part in His mysterious ways.

CARRIE

Journal entry, June 13, 2007 (her final entry following the death of Matt and less than three weeks before her own death): In this journal entry, I would like to share another one of Bob Sorge's secrets [paraphrases from Secrets of the Secret Place, *chapter 32 – The Secret of Waiting]. We wait. We wait for our hearts to hurt less, we wait to feel some strength again, we wait for this cancer that we believe is being healed to manifest the healing and that the miracle will be completed with restoration, and we wait for God to continue to show us how He desires to fulfill His purposes through us here on earth. Waiting is hard; it is tedious and it is something the enemy uses to discourage us because he wants to wear us down and out as we wait. The enemy cannot have us— WILL NOT have us. We are in the arms of Jesus; we are confined to His arms and His safety. We pray that whatever this day brings for you, that you will experience this love and safety as well. Oh, we hope that for you. One does not have to go through cancer and the death of a child to feel in confinement. Be at peace in His arms and allow your heart to beat softly and slowly as you experience the love of Jesus in fresh, deep ways.*

After I typed the words from Carrie's journal entry, I opened my own copy of *Secrets of the Secret Place* to chapter 47, "The Secret of Clinging." I really related to this today because I found myself clinging to Jesus throughout the long night, and then turning to Him this morning in worship and prayer. I told Him how I hate that my son is suffering, and He reminded me that He suffered for all of us and is with us even now. His words in John 15:5 resonated with truth: "Apart from Me, you can do nothing."

Bob Sorge writes, "I used to think that Christian maturity meant that we got stronger and stronger until we were an intimidat-

ing force to be reckoned with by the powers of darkness. But the
image of maturity that's given for us in Scripture is quite different
from that." He goes on a few paragraphs later to attest to the power
of clinging to His word:

> I clutch His word to my breast as though it is my very
> life. "I cling to Your testimonies; O Lord, do not put
> me to shame!" (Psalm 119:31) I think that "testimo-
> nies" point, in part, to the stories of God's mighty acts
> of intervention on behalf of the saints of history—
> how He parted the waters; how He fed them with
> manna; how He leveled the walls of Jericho; how He
> raised the dead to life. These are His testimonies, and
> they reflect His ways—how He handles His devout
> ones who love Him. I cling to the stories of God's
> power revealed because they encourage me that He
> still works in the same magnificent ways today. I cling
> to His testimonies for I need that same miraculous
> power to be released in my own life.[16]

Our Paul has seen one testimony after another of healing,
restoration, and hope fulfilled. He has seen me rise, take up my
mat, and walk again. He has seen his own broken body put back
together after a nearly catastrophic bicycle accident last Halloween.
He has seen his father continue to lift the name of Jesus on high
in the midst of the suffering of his family, and to provide tender
nurturing for the duration. He has seen God's hand of provision
bring new life to his sponsored "brother" Stephen in Uganda. He
has just begun to see the goodness of the Lord in the land of the
living. It is all and always by the blood of Jesus.

Nothing is too difficult for our awesome God—and nothing
can separate us from His love that is in Christ Jesus. Our Paul takes
his name from one who learned that through countless personal
testimonies of God's abiding faithfulness: the apostle Paul. "For I
am convinced that neither death nor life, neither angels nor demons,
neither the present nor the future, nor any powers, neither height

nor depth, nor anything else in all creation will be able to separate us from the love of God that is in Christ Jesus" (Romans 8:38-39). That includes cancer or any other disease. That is a promise.

As I took my daily walk around the pond (well, it's really a glorified drainage ditch), I allowed the Holy Spirit to bring to my heart some of the old songs and hymns I had memorized in my youth. I am ever so thankful for the gift of these words that are forever hidden in my heart. What emerged from my voice this morning were words from the hymn, "How Firm a Foundation:"

> Fear not, I am with thee—O be not dismayed,
> For I am thy God and will still give thee aid;
> I'll strengthen thee, help thee, and cause thee to stand,
> Upheld by my gracious, omnipotent hand.

> When through the deep waters I call thee to go,
> The rivers of woe shall not thee overflow;
> For I will be with thee thy troubles to bless,
> And sanctify to thee thy deepest distress.

> The soul that on Jesus hath leaned for repose,
> I will not, I will not desert to his foes;
> That soul, tho' all hell should endeavor to shake,
> I'll never—no, never—no, never forsake.

Gracious and holy God, what comfort it gives us to cling to you and your promises! Thank you for your Word of truth and for the abiding love of Jesus that will never desert us to our foes. We wait for you with confidence, Lord, knowing that you who promised are faithful and will teach us the ways in which we should go. We pray in Jesus' name, Amen.

Therefore go and make disciples of all nations, baptizing them in the name of the Father and of the Son and of the Holy Spirit, and teaching them to obey everything I have commanded you. And surely I will be with you always, to the very end of the age. —Matthew 28:19

18

Mentoring

"So what exactly does 'Mentor' mean?" The wedding pho-tographers were attempting to fulfill their quota of pictures for every member of the bridal party listed in the program for the marriage ceremony of Hannah Nelson and Mike Lu on Saturday, June 28, 2008, and since Hannah had designated me as "Mentor and Vocal Coach of the Bride," one of them thought she'd better find out to what species "Mentor" belonged. The wedding coordina-tor, a young woman named Rebekah, explained to them that I was one of Hannah's professors at Rice and had been asked by her to provide guidance and encouragement in various life concerns and spiritual matters. To me, this relationship represents one of the most rewarding roles a Christian can fulfill in life and fulfills the biblical admonition of Paul to Titus in Titus 2:3-4: "Teach the older women to be reverent in the way they live, not to be slanderers or addicted to much wine, but to teach what is good. Then they can train the younger women…"

As I reflect on my own personal development, I can recall many who have helped me along the paths of life, but few whom I would consider true mentors. So what is the difference? To me, a mentor is one who helps another to "grasp how wide and long and high and deep is the love of Christ, and to know this love that surpasses knowledge—that you may be filled to the measure of all the fullness of God" (Ephesians 3:18-19).

Our first mentors are, hopefully, our parents. Mine certainly were, and my mom, at a vibrant age eighty-two, still is. They labored for the Kingdom of God first in the pastorate and then as lay leaders in retirement. They modeled lives that were committed to the call of Christ through serving others. I observed the seemingly endless ways in which they were His hands, His feet, His ears, His voice—and His heart. I wanted to be like them.

My Grandma Grace was a mentor to me through a life that was so simple and selfless. She married my grandfather, a widower, when she was fifty-four, and embraced our ready-made family as her own. Since I was still a baby, she was the only grandma I ever knew. Her very life preached the gospel of Christ without words, in the manner of St. Francis of Assisi. She simply followed Jesus' admonition to "love one another as I have first loved you." She gave me a lavish awareness of who Jesus is. Her life bore abundant fruit. She lived up to her name: Grace. I wanted to be like her.

As I grew in my Christian walk, the Lord provided many women to model the way for me. Although I had never asked anyone to formally serve as a mentor to me, they just seemed to appear almost like angels when I needed this kind of guidance. I had wandered from my faith in college and married outside of the will of God in my twenties. As I was going through an extremely painful divorce, the Lord sent to me a sweet woman named Shirley Rollins. She was a singer and had come for vocal coaching, but she served as an ad hoc spiritual coach to me, always feeding me with the living Word. Shirley was a kidney transplant recipient and walked through some pretty significant trials, including the death of her daughter Robin from breast cancer, but emerged as more than a conqueror. She was the one who gave me my first copy of Oswald Chambers' devotional classic, *My Utmost for His Highest*. I feasted on this book until I wore it out (and now I'm exhausting my second copy)! Shirley understood his very words on discipleship in the entry from April 24th:

> Our work begins where God's grace has laid the foundation; we are not to save souls, but to disciple them. Salvation and sanctification are the work of God's sovereign grace; our work as His disciples is to disciple lives until they are wholly yielded to God. One life wholly devoted to God is of more value to God than one hundred lives simply awakened by His Spirit. As workers for God we must reproduce our own kind spiritually, and that will be God's witness to us as workers. God brings us to a standard of life by His grace, and we are responsible for reproducing that standard in others.[17]

Another God-supplied mentor was my dear friend Irene Friedlob, who was also a coaching student of mine in Denver. Funny how the Lord brought godly women right to my doorstep when I needed them most! Irene and her husband Ray welcomed me into their home during my divorce proceedings, and it was through Irene's gentle love and continuous affirmation that I eventually found my way back to the Lord and then met Philippe. She was the one I called to be with me on that dark day in May, 1990, when I heard the dreaded words from Dr. Cedars: "You have cancer." She was the one who made herself available to take me to the endless round of medical appointments before and after my surgery. She and Ray rejoiced with Philippe and me when we adopted Paul, and have served as his loving godparents ever since. She reproduced God's standard of life in me by His grace.

Barb Roberts, Director of Caring Ministry at our church in Denver, also played a vital role in mentoring me through cancer, the loss of our children, and my dad's death from prostate cancer. Barb taught me so much about the priceless gift of presence: just showing up. A woman of great wisdom and love, God has given her the ability to know when to speak and when to simply sit and be still, knowing that He is God. My most poignant recollection of Barb was on a frigid Sunday morning, February 10 of 2002, when she appeared at 7:30 a.m. at the door to my dad's hospice room. I had kept vigil with him throughout the night as his earthly life waned; my body was weary and my spirit cried out to the Lord for sustenance. Seeing Barb with a platter of warm homemade caramel pecan rolls just about convinced me that I had gone to heaven! She taught me how to love as Jesus does.

After my cancer diagnosis and surgery in 1990, I had to face the fact that I would never bear biological children. As huge as that loss and consequent grief were, I didn't factor God's largesse into the equation. I never imagined that He would not only give us our precious adopted son Paul, but that He would also allow me to have countless spiritual sons and daughters through mentoring. The words from Isaiah 54:1 speak to my heart: "Sing, O barren woman, you who never bore a child; burst into song, shout for joy, you who were never in labor; because more are the children of the desolate woman than of her who has a husband." Obviously, I have a magnificent husband, Philippe—but I certainly qualified as a desolate woman for a while!

My position as Artist Teacher of Opera Studies at Rice is really the "excuse" for my purpose there: to share God's love and disciple others, both young men and women, in Christ. I count it pure joy to be in a secular environment, teaching classes as well as working with students one on one, and seeing the fruit of God's promise that His word will not return void, but will accomplish the purpose for which He sent it. I love watching these young lives seek His truth and find His love, and am so honored when they ask me to serve in this way. I embrace the role of mentor as the call of Christ.

It was only after his death in 2002 that I learned that Dr. Michael Hammond, former Dean of the Shepherd School at Rice, had been a peer mentor in the Anderson Network program at M.D.

Anderson Cancer Center, the same hospital where Carrie would eventually be treated and the primary venue for the flowering of our friendship. Dean Hammond battled pancreatic cancer for fourteen years, but had served as a volunteer to help others who had been diagnosed with the same type of cancer through encouraging them on this difficult journey.

When I learned of this program, I called the Anderson Network and applied to be a volunteer mentor. I have had the opportunity to interact with many women over the years who had received a similar diagnosis to mine, and to help them persevere with hope as they listened to my stories of God's provision. Just this last Christmas, I received a card from the first patient I had mentored several years ago, a woman named Pat in Ohio, who assured me that she would never forget the kindness and encouragement she felt during that time. Another patient, a beautiful young woman named Genevieve, later became a volunteer for the Anderson Network herself.

I often met with Carrie after my Rice classes on Tuesdays when she would be at M.D. Anderson for checkups and procedures. The campus is only a couple of miles from the hospital, so I'd drive over and meet her, generally on the 7th floor in Digestive Disorders, and we'd share the latest. She would often speak of young women she was mentoring, both formally and informally. She absolutely loved telling me all about her "daughter-in-love," Amy, who I know considered Carrie to be a very special mentor. So did Erin Smalley, who co-authored *Grown-Up Girlfriends* with Carrie. Erin writes in her chapter titled "The Grown-Up Friend Passes on What She Knows:"

> (Mentoring) is a relationship in which one person empowers another by sharing her experiences, gifts, and time. The key to mentoring is realizing that God has given each of us experiences and knowledge to share with other women. He knows who we should be passing on our wisdom to—we just need to ask for

His leading so we don't miss a golden opportunity to impact another woman. Carrie has served as my informal mentor over the years. She views our relationship as being 'fellow journeyers.' And truly, that is what being a mentor is: sharing the journey that the Lord has laid before both of you within the relationship. Life experience is a precious gift to share with another woman. The blessings the Lord gives through these opportunities are immeasurable.[18]

Even though I was initially "appointed" by our pastor to help Carrie through pancreatic cancer, she ended up serving as a mentor to me as well. I observed her steadfast faithfulness to the Lord in every circumstance; I watched how she loved with the love of Christ all who were placed in her path; I witnessed the growth of His presence in her even as her body withered and began to fade. I experienced the power of God's love that poured out like rivers of living water through her. I knew Him more because she lived. And the mentoring of Carrie's life and God-given wisdom continues even now through the lives she touched and through the pages of this book. To God be the glory; great things He has done!

Loving heavenly Father, You taught us how to love through your Son, Jesus Christ, and modeled mentoring through how He taught His disciples. Help us to share this same love with those that you bring into our lives, Lord, so that we can indeed fulfill your Great Commission to make disciples of all nations. We ask this in Jesus' name, and for His glory, Amen.

Trust in the Lord with all your heart and lean not on your own understanding; in all your ways acknowledge Him, and He will make your paths straight. —Proverbs 3:5-6

19

Trust

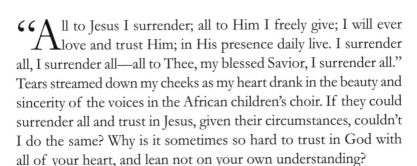

" All to Jesus I surrender; all to Him I freely give; I will ever love and trust Him; in His presence daily live. I surrender all, I surrender all—all to Thee, my blessed Savior, I surrender all." Tears streamed down my cheeks as my heart drank in the beauty and sincerity of the voices in the African children's choir. If they could surrender all and trust in Jesus, given their circumstances, couldn't I do the same? Why is it sometimes so hard to trust in God with all of your heart, and lean not on your own understanding?

My eighth-grade Sunday school teacher, Pauline Whitacre, gave me a plaque with that very scripture which I kept on my desk for years. Admittedly, it was soon memorized as head knowledge, but didn't really take root in my heart for many years. My first real challenge came when I had just begun my sophomore year at Northwestern University in Evanston, Illinois, and awakened in the middle of the night with extreme pain in my right knee. I hobbled down the hall to the restroom, took a couple of Tylenol, and went back to bed. When I could hardly walk the next morning, I knew it was time to hit the infirmary. They immediately put me in isolation and started running tests. I grew more and more ill, and on the third day, the doctor told my mom that I had been bitten by a brown recluse spider. There was no antitoxin, and my body was too weak to administer steroids, so all we could do was to wait—and pray—and trust in God.

As I lay in the dark one night in my private room, feeling my strength ebb away, I began to sense the company and ineffable comfort of the Lord surrounding me and knew I was truly not alone. I surrendered my will to Him and trusted that He would be with me. I also knew that many were praying. The next morning, the doctor stood amazed by my bedside as he examined the wound. It had healed overnight, bypassing the necrosis that is characteristic of that spider bite. There was no explanation other than God's healing hand at work in response to the prayers of His people. I was beginning to see that He is worthy of my trust—always.

CARRIE

Journal entry, June 26, 2005: We were created to live in the present. When we dare to trust that we are never alone but that God is always with us, always cares for us, and always speaks to us, then we can gradually detach ourselves from the voices that make us guilty or anxious and thus allow ourselves to dwell in the present moment. If I am living in the present, it is hard for that fear to kick in. I heard several wonderful stories of people surviving hard cancers this week and I heard some stories of people that have not survived. What do you do with all of this? You walk the moment, you hug harder than you usually do, you look into the eyes of people wherever you go, and you ask God to make you present to them. You trust. One of the hardest endeavors of humankind is to trust. To really trust that God is at work in my life in the way that He so chooses, in this here and for now.

One of the many characteristics that Carrie and I had in common was a tendency to want to be in control. One evening around 9:30 as she, Gary and I were leaving the parking garage at M.D. Anderson (the place that never sleeps!) after a long day of tests, I was navigating the maze of arrows and "One Way" signs, trying to get to the cashier. Carrie pointed to a "Do Not Enter" sign and said, "Take that way." My follow-the-rules inner child resisted until I glanced at Gary, who said with a wry grin, "Do as she says."

Cancer patients learn very quickly that there is a limit to what we can control. Neither Carrie nor I had done anything to "deserve" cancer; we both had low risk factors, ate well and exercised, so even the doctors were surprised by our diagnoses. Because we live in a fallen world, sometimes the inexplicable happens.

The good news is that we know that our God is always trustworthy. Even when we go through trials that seem like those of Job, we can say as he did, "Though He slay me, yet will I trust in Him" (Job 13:15). God is at work in every situation to bring redemption from those things that are rooted in evil. He is working to achieve in us an eternal glory that far outweighs these light and momentary troubles, according to II Corinthians 4:17, although they never seem light or momentary when they happen to you!

I love the Psalms of David for their transparency; he doesn't have a need to sugarcoat the emotions he brings before the Lord in the midst of distress:

How long, O Lord? Will you forget me forever?
How long will you hide your face from me?
How long must I wrestle with my thoughts
And every day have sorrow in my heart?
How long will my enemy triumph over me?
Look on me and answer, O Lord my God,
Give light to my eyes, or I will sleep in death;
My enemy will say, "I have overcome him,"
And my foes will rejoice when I fall.
But I trust in your unfailing love;
My heart rejoices in your salvation.
I will sing to the Lord,
For He has been good to me (Psalm 13).

CARRIE

Journal entry, March 10, 2007: I have already had to surrender many times over. My stomach has been worse since returning from Houston. The fluid does not seem to be draining. I am sad. I am disappointed and frustrated. I have no clothes that fit. My (size) 0's don't fit over the stomach. We joke that I look like an anorexic pregnant lady. I want that fixed. I can't think of anything along the way that has been more frustrating than this predicament. Nausea, diarrhea, radiation, you name it, does not rate up there with this protruding stomach. It gets downright uncomfortable, and the thing is I need to eat, but it makes me not want to eat. Not enough room!

*   I surrender, God. I surrender. I also keep trusting and hoping and believing and know that Easter is coming. I have said before that a precious intercessor was praying over me early on after the diagnosis in 2005, and she prayed that I would not focus on symptoms and be frightened by them. I have never forgotten that prayer. She, too, had walked through cancer. I go to bed at night and I check every morning to see if this stomach has gone down, because I believe that it will. Please believe with me. The cancer cannot have me. It just can't, and yet I surrender to my God, to what He is doing in my life.*

*   In these six weeks, I will watch my pansies grow, will finish a book with Gary, [*Mad About Us*] and will wait expectantly for a continued working of the Lord's hand. I will surrender. I will enjoy friendship, will walk and lift and breathe. I will go to church on Easter and I will rejoice because it is a year later from when I sat in the Pavilion in The Woodlands, and I will continue to expectantly wait on the Lord for the miracle I am asking Him for.*

Carrie trusted in God enough to tell Him exactly how she was feeling about the things that troubled her, and yet like David in Psalm 13, she always affirmed God's goodness and trustworthiness. I learned so much through her candor, as I had tried so hard during my own trials to not "dishonor" God by keeping my negative feelings to myself, mistakenly thinking that I was protecting His reputation! I've learned that He is more than able to defend Himself. I've also learned that one of the secrets to an intimate relationship with my heavenly Father is to tell Him everything that is on my heart; I do not need to edit or censor my prayers!

Jeremiah, the "weeping prophet," certainly didn't hold back from the full expression of his emotions. His inspired words recorded in Lamentations 3 minister to my spirit:

> I remember my affliction and my wandering, the bitterness and the gall. I well remember them, and my soul is downcast within me. Yet this I call to mind and therefore I have hope: Because of the LORD's great love we are not consumed, for his compassions never fail. They are new every morning; great is your faithfulness. I say to myself, "The LORD is my portion; therefore I will wait for him." The LORD is good to those whose hope is in him, to the one who seeks him... (Lamentations 3:19-25).

Another saint who has gone to Glory, the poetess and hymn writer Fanny Crosby, encountered her share of grief in life. Blinded at the age of six weeks through improper medical treatment, she went on to marry another blind musician, but lost their only child in early infancy. Despite it all, she went on to write between eight and nine thousand gospel hymn texts in the hope of evangelizing a million souls to Christ during the span of her life.

Just after I had received my cancer diagnosis in 1990, we were at the Saturday Sabbath service at our church in Denver, and we stood to sing Fanny Crosby's hymn "Blessed Assurance." Oh, how I needed to say those words, particularly the third verse:

> Perfect submission—all is at rest,
> I in my Savior am happy and blest;
> Watching and waiting, looking above,
> filled with His goodness, lost in His love.
> This is my story, this is my song,
> praising my Savior all the day long;
> this is my story, this is my song,
> praising my Savior all the day long.

I wept with those tears that only the Lord truly understands, offering them in surrender and with trust. This is my story. This is also Carrie's story. And He is our song, now and forever.

> **Precious Lord**, it is so good to trust in you; to know that we can lay our burdens at your feet and count on your mercies that are new every morning. You accept us just as we are—angry or glad, weak or strong, sick or well, and you supply all that we need. Thank you for your faithfulness. In Jesus' name, Amen.

This is love; not that we loved God, but that He loved us and sent His Son as an atoning sacrifice for our sins. Dear friends, since God so loved us, we also ought to love one another. No one has ever seen God; but if we love each other, God lives in us and His love is made complete in us.
—I John 4:10-12

20

Right Relationship

CARRIE
Journal entry, November 14, 2005: I have written about relationships in almost every journal entry on some level, but as I write this entry, I have to go deeper, go further—go where Christ has been working in my life in the last two weeks.

While I would say I have walked closely with Jesus most of my adult years, the verse that talks about Him saying, "Be gone from me, for I never knew you" has definitely gotten my attention in the past. It has been a motivator for me, but perhaps more out of fear that He could say those words to me if I didn't know Him enough, or if I missed something about knowing Him. I don't feel that way anymore. Is that because of the cancer journey? Perhaps. What I know abundantly, deeply, profoundly more than I used to know is the love and heart of the Father and the Son. I know this through the Word, through worship, and especially through the love of others in my life.

It occurred to me as I was mulling over this chapter of the book that Dr. Gary Oliver is the Executive Director of The Center for Relationship Enrichment at John Brown University, and Carrie served as the director of the University Relationships Initiative under those auspices. Two veritable relationship experts! Not only that, but they wrote books together (*Raising Sons and Loving It!* and *Mad About Us: Moving from Anger to Intimacy with Your Spouse*), traveled the country sharing their expertise and practical experience in marriage seminars, and had private counseling practices. No wonder I learned so much from them! However, the real proof was in the love of Christ that they extended to one another, to their family, to their friends and colleagues, and to everyone that God placed in their lives.

Our Creator fashioned us for relationship with Him, making us in His own image, and then gave us free will to choose the extent to which we would walk in His ways, delight in Him, and love Him. When we showed that we were all like sheep gone astray, He provided His only begotten Son, Jesus Christ, to be the sacrificial Lamb who died for our sins so that we might live in eternal relationship with God in His Kingdom. But we need right relationship both with Him and with those in this world so that we might be conformed to the image of Christ and further His Kingdom on earth as it is in heaven. "We love because He first loved us. If anyone says, 'I love God', yet hates his brother, he is a liar. For anyone who does not love his brother, whom he has seen, cannot love God, whom he has not seen. And He has given us this command: Whoever loves God must also love his brother" (I John 4:19-21).

If God's mandate is to love one another, it is essential that we learn how to forgive, for we can't possibly show love to those for whom we feel enmity. Just as sin separates us from God and we are reconciled through the atoning blood of Jesus to receive God's forgiveness when we earnestly repent, so we must extend and receive forgiveness from all with whom we are in relationship, particularly with our spouses. In the Olivers' book *Mad About Us*, they write on the topic of forgiveness in chapter 11:

> One of the key components of intimacy is the ability to forgive and to ask for forgiveness. Forgiveness is essential in order for any relationship to keep growing

and for trust to deepen or to be reestablished if broken. Forgiveness is the avenue, the path that we must walk down if we are to let go of anger, resentment, and negativity toward our spouse, which almost always hinders intimacy.[19]

If our marital relationship is to model Christ as the bridegroom and His church as the bride, we must certainly come to understand that His forgiveness of our sins is also what we are to extend to one another. Gary and Carrie elaborate on this on page 172 of their book:

> For many, coming to Christ is the first real awareness of the need for forgiveness. We come to believe that Jesus Christ truly died for our sin. We may picture our sin as the worst, or we may think we are okay (really we have not done anything too bad.) "There are many who have done so much more than I have sin-wise," we tell ourselves. We can carry this mentality into our marriage and hurt the level of trust our spouse has in us if we are unwilling to take responsibility for even the smallest wrongs toward our beloved. Forgiveness is the healing balm that keeps a relationship vibrant and growing. Forgiveness propels us forward. A lack of forgiveness often keeps us wounded and stuck in the past.[20]

I had been asked to speak to a group of young women at our church last week on the topic of forgiveness, and after diligently (sometimes dutifully!) preparing for weeks, I sat down at my computer and pounded out several pages of notes. Satisfied that I had enough material to fill forty-five minutes, I printed it and smugly filed it away until the next day. However, the Lord has taught me to hold these things very loosely; it's almost as if He says, "The preparation was for you, dear one; now I will tell you what I want them to hear."

Imagine my astonishment when the Holy Spirit showed me

Leviticus 7 early the next morning and I was utterly convicted that I was to teach on the concept of the "guilt offering." I protested a little, but sensed the Lord telling me that His children needed to understand the Old Covenant in order to truly comprehend the sacrificial Gift of His Son, Jesus. Then I was led to the New Testament book of Hebrews, chapters eight through ten: the summation of the New Covenant! My body trembled with awe and anticipation as I contemplated the wonder of it all. God reconciled us to Him once—and for all—by the blood of Jesus. NOTHING BUT THE BLOOD OF JESUS!

Having little time to devote to the reconfiguration of my talk, I simply surrendered to the One "who is able to do exceedingly abundantly more than we can ask or even imagine according to His power that is at work within us" (Ephesians 3:20). But it got even harder! I felt the Lord impress on me that I was to share my own struggle to forgive others, along with some highly emotional testimonies from my life. Zounds! The reason was clarified by the passage from Hebrews 10:23-25:

> Let us hold unswervingly to the hope we profess, for He who promised is faithful. And let us consider how we may spur one another on toward love and good deeds. Let us not give up meeting together, as some are in the habit of doing, but let us encourage one another—and all the more as you see the Day approaching.

Forgiveness through the blood of Jesus equals right relationship, both with God and with one another. I received my marching orders for that day, and my Commander-in-Chief saw me through!

Life on earth is brief at best; in the words of an old hymn, "A thousand ages in Thy sight are like an evening gone." Those of us who have become more acutely aware of its brevity through our own experience with cancer or the loss of a loved one (or in many cases, as with Gary Oliver, both) have a bit of an edge, perhaps, because we often begin to embrace life more fully. There is a definitive moment for many of us when we choose either to trust God and enter into the most profound relationship there is, or retreat in anger, grief, or even disbelief. If we move forward in the knowledge that "He who promised is faithful," God enlarges our lives and reveals Himself in unprecedented ways. Every relationship grows richer as a result, and we seek ways in which we can show the love of Christ to others.

Carrie and I were kindred spirits in this awareness of God's love and His power to transform what some might consider torture into an opportunity to grow in Him and extend His love to others. When we'd rendezvous on the 7th floor at M.D. Anderson for her appointments, she would eagerly tell me stories of her new friends (not ever just acquaintances, always friends!) who had perhaps read her journal, sat next to her during chemo, or even served as her nurses, doctors, or technicians. How she loved people! She would minister to them even in the midst of the greatest trial of her life. She loved them with the love of Jesus.

CARRIE

Journal entry, November 13, 2006: Before cancer, I don't think I would have readily signed up for pain and suffering, like "Bring it on, God!" Nope, none of us, if we are brutally honest, really grasp God's incredible love that allows us to suffer. When we do encounter pain, it is at that point we meet His incredible love, His grace, and mercy in ways that sustain us and keep us breathing even at the points we feel we can't anymore. That is deep, deep love. That is a love that I look for almost every day working in my life now. I have to. It is my oxygen, and without it, I cannot live. Funny, I thought I was really living before! Suffering is a crossroad for us humans, I suppose. It is a place where we choose to be loved in deeper ways or we choose to fight with anger, depression, or just plain sinful behavior.

I am thankful for the whole concept of love. I don't really want to sign up for any more furnace experiences, and I don't really want to die, but I know I can't live without the Father's love, however He chooses to demonstrate that love for me. I am glad that His promises are true and that ultimately, I can trust my Lord for everything this world has to offer me, both wonderful and difficult.

"Ultimately, I can trust my Lord for everything this world has to offer me, both wonderful and difficult." Carrie's words exemplify trusting in the Lord and leaning not unto our own understanding. She trusted in His perfect plan and now she is wearing His crown of righteousness in the company of the other saints of the ages. It gives me such inexpressible joy to contemplate these relationships awaiting us in heaven! I live to hear Jesus say, "Come, you who are blessed by my Father, take your inheritance, the Kingdom prepared for you since the creation of the world." I imagine meeting our precious unborn twins for the first time! I think of the great figures of the Bible like Abraham, Job, David, Daniel, John, Paul; the martyrs, too many to count; composers like J.S. Bach, George Frideric Handel and Felix Mendelssohn, who truly loved and served the Lord; my own father, Norman Herbert, and my sister, Jennifer; dear grandparents, aunts and uncles; some close friends, especially young Zack Homrighaus; precious, precious Carrie and her dear son, Matt. All living abundant life in relationship with Jesus and one another, waiting to welcome all who call Him Savior and Lord.

CARRIE

Journal entry, November 14, 2005: I am thankful to know Jesus, and have come to know Him more deeply through my earthly relationships. When I meet Him face to face, there is no doubt that He will say to me, "Come to Me, little one, for I know you well!" And we will embrace and perhaps, just maybe, we shall even dance together.

Precious Lord, what incomparable joy it is to know that you created us to enjoy an eternal relationship with you! Thank you for the redeeming blood of Jesus that has allowed us to know that our future in heaven is secure when we ask Christ to be our Savior. Help us to be like Him while we are still living in this world, to love one another as He first loved us, so that you may be glorified on earth as you are in Heaven. We ask in Jesus' name, Amen.

Though He brings grief, He will show compassion, so great is His unfailing love. For He does not willingly bring affliction or grief to the children of men. —Lamentations 3:32-33

21

Grief

The announcement came in the mail yesterday, which was also the first anniversary of Carrie's death, July 2, 2008: "BABY ARRIVAL—We are tickled pink to announce the birth of our daughter, Alivia Merrell Oliver…" I couldn't help but think that this was God's perfect timing and evidence that He brings a crown of beauty from ashes, the oil of gladness instead of mourning, and a garment of praise for a spirit of despair (Isaiah 61:3). Even as I regard the picture of this precious new little one, I see a gaze that reminds me of her grandmother, Carrie. We have all survived the first year of grief, and God has brought new life to the Oliver family.

Grief is such a strange and personal thing that manifests itself in unique ways with each encounter. I have long been familiar with the five stages of grief delineated by Elisabeth Kübler-Ross in her book published in 1969, *On Death and Dying*: denial, anger, bargaining, depression, and acceptance. Ross maintained that everyone would go through at least two of these stages in the grief process; some would go through all five—but not necessarily in that order.[21]

I have had to navigate the roiling waters of grief many, many times thus far, but hardly consider myself an expert. What has continued to perplex me is that each time feels as though I haven't been there before! As I contemplated this phenomenon in my attempt to put it into words, I had to consider what constitutes "grief" in the first place. It always seems to involve a loss with subsequent change, but isn't always provoked by something tragic. In fact, one can experience grief after a wedding! Perhaps one of the reasons newlyweds often have a challenging first year is that their individual expectations are higher than their spouse can fulfill; their new status as a couple also involves relinquishing some autonomy. The old freedom is gone, and it must be grieved as a loss before the new identity as a couple can be firmly established.

Grief can result from any type of loss, from as mundane as losing a wallet to as profound as the diagnosis of cancer or the death of a spouse or child. It is curious to me that the world finds it easier to deal with those who are experiencing the former—and would just as soon avoid encounters with the latter. People are fairly comfortable empathizing with material losses because most of us have experienced that at one time or another. Even job losses or divorces have become more and more commonplace, so they're within the realm of shared experience.

My first truly profound encounter with grief came after the loss of our babies in early pregnancy in April of 1990, revealing the endometrial cancer which necessitated a total hysterectomy. Denial was my preferred stage and I lingered there for a long, long time. Because I didn't look sick or act sick, it was fairly easy to pretend that there wasn't anything that I couldn't deal with on my own over time. However, that cloak of denial demanded expression, and I felt myself moving into a deep depression. It was very threatening for me to acknowledge any anger, especially towards God, as I felt that it was contradictory to my belief in His goodness. I didn't understand the concept stated by Gary and Carrie Oliver in their book *Raising Sons and Loving It*:

Anger is an almost automatic response to any kind of pain, an emotion we feel almost immediately after we have been hurt...Through our expression of anger, God gets our attention and makes us aware of opportunities to learn, to grow, to mature, and to make significant changes for the good. Like love, anger has tremendous potential for both good and evil.[22]

My depression masked the anger stage as I turned it all inward.

God provided a resident counselor in the person of my dear husband, Philippe. Despite his own grief at the loss of our children and the death of our dream of bringing new life into the world, he gently and ever so patiently kept speaking truth —God's truth— into the situation. He encouraged me to speak of my fears so that with God's help, they could be banished. He held me and told me I was beautiful when I felt like the female version of a eunuch. He willingly pursued adoption so that we could one day be parents. He was like Jesus to me. Acceptance came.

The death of my dad from prostate cancer on February 10, 2002 was an entirely different grief experience. Since Dad had become ill the day before the collapse of the twin towers at the World Trade Center on September 11, 2001, we were all dealing with a time of great uncertainty in our country, compounding the distress we felt over his illness. However, we gathered around him and expressed emotions that had never seen the light of day in our family. This became a time of liberation for me as I saw aspects of my dad I never realized were there. As he became more ill, I knew his time was limited and was determined to make the most of every moment we had together. I had never initiated prayer with Dad; after all, he was the ordained pastor and I was only a praying lay minister! But the Holy Spirit nudged me until I complied, and it opened up a new and glorious gift from God to both of us. I had the privilege of being at his bedside, along with my dear mom, when he uttered a last cry of victory and passed into the arms of

Jesus. So much of the grief process had been already traversed that it was truly a time of glory.

The unexpected death of my sister Jennifer on July 18, 2004, was an event that truly rocked my world. The phone message from my mom late on that Sunday afternoon was frantic: "Jennifer has committed suicide!" My reaction was like that of a wild animal snared by a hunter's trap from which there would be no release. A primal scream emitted from what seemed to be my disembodied throat. Our worst fears had materialized.

Jennifer had been gradually declining since the death of our father two and a half years before. Afflicted by a form of autism known as Asperger's Syndrome, she had always dealt with limited social skills and had retreated into isolation, later complicated by physical pain and increasingly frequent psychotic episodes. We had sought treatment for her and she had seemed to improve for a time after hospitalization, but she simply could not cope with her life on earth. She knew Jesus as her Savior and had allowed me to share scriptures with her and pray frequently over the phone, but she expressed tremendous fear at the prospect of managing life on a daily basis.

This venture into grief was definitely uncharted territory for me and for my family. My first coping mechanism was to be like the biblical Martha, handling the immediate practical needs that arose with the crisis: making funeral arrangements, cleaning out her apartment, planning the memorial service. Step two was to lose myself in my music, a lifelong escape, by producing a CD of hymns and classical music that I played on the piano as a memorial to Jennifer. Step three involved helping my mom move from Colorado to Illinois so that she would be near extended family again. It wasn't until the following fall that I actually encountered my grief.

I was walking past the office in our church that sunny Wednesday morning in October, 2005, when Pastor Stew Grant looked at me quizzically through the window. He motioned for me to wait and came out into the hall a moment later, saying, "Are you alright?"

"Sure!" I replied. "We just finished Bible study and it was great." Looking at me with his kind and discerning eyes, he persisted. "No, I mean, are you REALLY alright?" Well, the floodgates opened as my tightly-maintained façade crumbled before both of us. He ushered me into a conference room and let me sob. Then he explained to me that I had immense grief to deal with and that I needed help. He recommended a wonderful licensed Christian counselor, Cindy Littlefield, and also assured me that he would meet with me for several sessions in the interim.

God so clearly provided what I didn't even realize I needed. There I was, still stuck in denial mode after fifteen months! I couldn't find the way out of the maze of grief on my own, but God did an Isaiah 65:24, "Before they call I will answer." He led me to exactly the right sources of help without my even asking. "The Lord my God shall supply all of my need according to His riches in glory in Christ Jesus" (Philippians 4:19).

One of the reasons I hadn't progressed further than the first stage of grief was that society finds any mention of suicide abhorrent and nearly reprehensible. I almost felt like I was a leper who needed to announce myself by shouting "Unclean! Unclean!" Most people were so obviously uncomfortable that it became easier to just say that I was doing alright than to try to express my true thoughts. This inability to make myself understood became its own kind of grief.

C.S. Lewis, in the book *A Grief Observed*, chronicled his own grief after the death of his wife, Joy, from cancer:

> No one ever told me that grief felt so like fear. I am not afraid, but the sensation is like being afraid. The same fluttering in the stomach, the same restlessness, the yawning. I keep on swallowing. At other times it feels like being mildly drunk, or concussed. There is a sort of invisible blanket between the world and me. I find it hard to take in what anyone says. Or perhaps, hard to want to take it in. It is so uninteresting. Yet I

want the others to be about me. I dread the moments when the house is empty. If only they would talk to one another and not to me. There are moments, most unexpectedly, when something inside me tries to assure me that I don't really mind so much, not so very much, after all. Love is not the whole of a man's life. I was happy before I ever met H. (his wife, Joy). I've plenty of what are called "resources." People get over these things. Come, I shan't do so badly. One is ashamed to listen to this voice but it seems for a little to be making out a good case. Then comes a sudden jab of red-hot memory and all this "commonsense" vanishes like an ant in the mouth of a furnace.[23]

Many of my grief experiences have involved physical sensations similar to those of Lewis. In fact, the summer after the death of my sister, I went through a period during which I completely lost my senses of smell and taste for a period of several weeks, and had episodes of obscured vision. Even after an MRI of my brain was assessed as normal, the symptoms persisted. I believe that it was my body's way of processing the grief that my mind could not yet absorb. It simply shut down and retreated like a turtle into its carapace. It took our awesome God working through Stew Grant and Cindy Littlefield to pull me back out.

Another phone call will be forever emblazoned in my memory. Carrie had called at 5:30 a.m. on Saturday, May 5, 2007. I didn't get her message until two hours later when I switched my cell phone on, but her voice had the same frenetic tone that my mother's had three years before. "Our son Matt is dead!" she sobbed. The trapped, wounded animal cry came out of my throat once again as I echoed her sobs. Another grief had begun.

CARRIE

Journal entry, June 13, 2007: The memorial service on May 9th will be one of those days in time we wish we would have never had to experience, and yet a day where we will never forget the hand of God on all of our family's lives, hearts, bodies and souls. We gave our son to the Lord that day to be held in His loving arms while we are left to figure out life here on this earth without him. I will talk more of that day when I can, but for now, it was a blessing and the most difficult day of my life.

(Carrie's journal, continued) We are now walking on the other side of the service, of a death several weeks from the event, with holes in our hearts—still battling cancer, working at our jobs, and Andrew finishing up school. Those initial days can be hell on earth that drive us straight to heaven. If we had not sought all that the heavenlies have to offer, we would not have made it. We would have given up on life, on love, on relationships, on God, on each other—and sunken deep into darkness. We are still in the light, even though we hurt.

Carrie's health declined very rapidly after Matt's death, and not even two months later, she joined him in heaven. I learned so much more about grief during this time, especially observing Gary Oliver. There was a transparency about his emotions that was so honest and straightforward; it made those of us who were also grieving give ourselves permission to express what was really on our hearts. Gary phoned Philippe and me on July 15, not even two weeks after Carrie's death, and with complete candor and without a trace of self-pity, said, "I hate my life right now, but I still love my Lord." That single sentence transformed my entire concept of grief.

Our Lord Himself grieved over the death of his friend Lazarus. We need to grieve over the loss of those whom we love and to feel that it is safe and acceptable to do so for however long it takes. Shortly after Carrie died, I began to experience a constriction in my throat, and then a period of several months when my voice would simply give out. This was not desirable for someone who works as a vocal coach! Looking back on my other walks through grief, I began to see the pattern: unexpressed grief coming out through my body. I told Philippe that I thought my physical problem was the result of grief over the loss of my precious friend. He agreed, and said, "It's almost as if in losing Carrie, you lost a voice...the voice of a friend with whom you had shared your heart." In verbalizing this, and in having it validated by the one closest to me, I was able to begin to move on in order to complete the grieving process.

The call to write this book, which the Lord had clearly impressed on both Carrie and me, has been another great gift from God and a catharsis for my grief. My voice has now been physically restored, but more importantly, Carrie's voice is being heard through the journaled legacy of her walk with God through the valley of the shadow of death into the brilliant light of His eternal presence. He is restoring the years the locusts have eaten. He is working all things together for good. He is bringing beauty from ashes. To God alone be the glory!

> **Our dear heavenly Father**, how comforting it is to know that you grieve right along with us and that you bottle our tears. Lord, I ask that you comfort those who are in the throes of grief even as they read this, and assure them with the knowledge that death has been swallowed up in the victory that is Christ. We pray this in Jesus' name, Amen.

As you come to Him, the living Stone—rejected by men but chosen by God and precious to Him—you also, like living stones, are being built into a spiritual house to be a holy priesthood, offering spiritual sacrifices acceptable to God through Jesus Christ. —I Peter 2:45

22

Sacrifice

Having been raised a Presbyterian, I was interested to read what John Calvin, the sixteenth-century theologian, had to say about living a life of sacrifice. In the book *Devotional Classics*, edited by Richard Foster and James Bryan Smith, one of my favorite anthologies of the writings of the saints throughout the ages, there is a chapter devoted to Calvin with excerpts from his *Golden Booklet of the True Christian Life*:

> It is the duty of believers to "present your bodies a living sacrifice, holy, acceptable unto God" (Romans 12:1); this is the only true worship. The principle of holiness leads to the exhortation, "Be not conformed to this world; but be ye transformed by the renewing of your mind, that ye may prove what is the will of God" (Romans 12:2). It is a very important consideration that we are consecrated and dedicated to God. It means that we will think, speak, meditate, and do all things with a view to God's glory.
>
> If we are not our own, but the Lord's, it is clear to what purpose all our deeds must be directed. We are not our

own, therefore neither our reason nor our will should guide us in our thoughts and actions. We are not our own, therefore we should not seek what is only expedient to the flesh. We are not our own, therefore let us forget ourselves and our own interests as far as possible. We are God's own; to Him therefore, let us live and die. We are God's own; therefore let His wisdom and will dominate all our actions. We are God's own; therefore let every part of our existence be directed towards Him as our only legitimate goal.[24]

It is utterly humbling for me to read those words and to become freshly aware of what sacrificial living is all about. There is actually a freedom that comes with the awareness that I am "not my own," but that I am a bondservant of the Lord Jesus Christ. If I live each day according to what Jesus told His disciples in Matthew 16:24, I am to deny myself, take up my cross, and follow Him. This puts order to my day, purpose to my life, and a reason for any and all of my suffering. Sometimes I go kicking and screaming, and I am definitely a work in progress, but I am beginning to see the light—His light.

God does not ordain suffering; He allows it in order to draw us nearer to Him and to accomplish Kingdom work in our lives. In this "me first" world in which we find ourselves, our sinful nature has become culturally acceptable as we strive to rise to the top. I am certainly the poster child for this, as I have been extraordinarily ambitious—and not always for the cause of Christ! One of the great daily devotionals that I have read over and over for many years is *Experiencing God Day-By-Day* by Henry and Richard Blackaby. In two excerpts from February 17th and 18th, they address this self-centeredness that has its root in the old nature:

Self-centered people try to keep their lives unruffled and undisturbed, safe and secure. Our temptation is to give our time and effort to the goals of this world. Then, when we are successful in the world's eyes, we seek to bring God into our world by honoring Him with our success. God is not interested in receiving secondhand glory from our activity. God receives glory from HIS activity through our lives. Your 'cross' is God's will for you, regardless of the cost. Taking up your cross is a choice; it is not beyond your control. You may have health problems or a rebellious child or financial pressures, but do not mistake these as your 'cross to bear.' Neither circumstances you face nor consequences of your own actions are your cross. Your cross will be to voluntarily participate in Christ's sufferings as he carries out His redemptive purposes (Philippians 3:10). There are aspects of God's redemptive work that can be accomplished only through suffering. Just as Christ had to suffer in order to bring salvation, there will be hardships you may have to endure in order for God to bring salvation to those around you.

There is no Christianity without a cross. If you are waiting for a relationship with God that never requires suffering or inconvenience, then you cannot use Christ as your model. God's will for you involves a cross. First, take up your cross, then you can follow Him.[25]

My life has been blessed by so many who have sacrificed for me because of their love for Jesus. Certainly my parents modeled this time and time again, both in their living and their giving. My dad retired from forty years in the ministry just two weeks after my cancer surgery, and my parents moved to Denver to be near Philippe and me. One evening as we were relaxing in our family room, they announced that they had a surprise for us. Their congregation at First Presbyterian Church in Waukegan, Illinois had presented them with a generous check at their retirement party, and instead of keeping it for their own use, they had endowed a scholarship fund at Trinity Evangelical Divinity School "in memory of the unborn de Chambrier children, to be awarded to the student who shows the most promise in child evangelism." I was simply blown away, as was my husband. This sacrificial gift so validated the suffering we had endured and memorialized the children we would only greet one day in heaven. We could not have asked for a greater expression of God's love.

My sister Jennifer also offered an enormous sacrifice in the name of Jesus. When she learned that there was a remote possibility that doctors at M.D. Anderson could do a procedure to stimulate my ovaries to produce eggs prior to the hysterectomy, she offered to be a surrogate mother for me, despite her own disability and the risk to herself. Although we then learned that I would not be a viable candidate for this, her willingness to sacrifice her own body to bear a child for me was a priceless gift.

We have had dear friends who have denied themselves and given sacrificially to us in His name; certainly there are too many to name them all. I think of my dear Irene and Ray Friedlob, who so gently nurtured me in their home for six weeks during the time of my divorce so many years ago; two special couples here in The Woodlands, the Bacons and the Winslows, who offered to drive me all the way from Texas to Denver, Colorado when my dad became so ill on September 11, 2001, and all air traffic had been halted, with Philippe stranded in Florida; beloved cousins Maggie and Mike, who visited Jennifer many times when she was in the hospital and we were too far away; our precious friends Lisa and Andy Norman, who drove all the way to Chicago from their vacation with family in Canada and Michigan to sort through Jennifer's apartment with us after her death; my dear friend Trish, who always seems to appear on our doorstep when I need her the most; my cherished prayer partner Camille in New Braunfels, always available to call on the Father together; Peggy and Rob Renfroe, frequent first-responders; the Rineharts in Tulsa, Philippe's "second" parents, who phoned when they heard about the impending Hurricane Rita and urged us to find shelter with them. All of these are bondservants of the

Lord Jesus Christ, yielded to His ways and following Him.

And then there is Philippe, who has poured himself out daily for me; my bridegroom who loves me with ongoing sacrificial love. I am humbled beyond description by memories of the times when he has taken my own suffering upon himself, spending nights cradling and comforting me when I have been wracked with pain, praying for me for hours at a time when I have not been able to sleep, and once keeping vigil at the foot of our bed for two hours when I was asleep to ask God to let me continue to sleep! The times when he has interrupted work (once when he had just pushed his plane back from the gate and was preparing for takeoff); times when he changed vacation plans at the last minute; the innumerable times when he tirelessly repeated words of faith and encouragement to me when I was faltering—I don't know what I would have done, or would do, without him.

Carrie and Gary were also paragons of self-denial and sacrifice. The last visit they made together to Houston was on June 18th, 2007—just six weeks after the death of their son, Matt, and two weeks before Carrie's death. As much as I wanted to deny it, she was very, very sick. However, the presence of Christ in both Gary and Carrie was so evident that the physical evidence of illness simply paled in comparison. As Gary and I sat in the waiting room for Carrie to have her CT scan, a man approached Gary and introduced himself as someone who had attended a Promise Keeper's conference and met Gary there (Gary served on the Board of Directors). This man was at M.D. Anderson with his wife, who had just been diagnosed with breast cancer. Gary gave them the fullness of his attention and then asked if he could pray for them, not even revealing his own circumstances until afterwards. This was the sacrificial love of Christ.

The Olivers stayed with us in The Woodlands during that visit, and I savor the memories of our last time together as couples. The second night was ominously dark and blustery, but they had made plans to meet their dear friends Sylvie and Ehab Hanna for dinner and were headed out into the wind and rain. Carrie didn't notice the four-inch step in our garage and plunged onto the concrete like a rag doll. As I screamed to the guys for help, I prayed for the Lord's hand on her. A moment later, she allowed Gary and Philippe to help her up, matter-of-factly brushed herself off, and stepped purposefully into the car. I said, "Carrie, maybe you should just stay home and rest," but she responded that there were some things—Kingdom things—she just had to share with the Hannas. She arose, took up her cross, and followed Him.

Gary speaks of these last days with Carrie in his audio message entitled "Sovereign Joy," which he delivered in Tampa, FL just four months after she died (http://www.liferelationships.com/). He relates the barrage of events that have threatened each member of his family over the past several years: his own battles with recurrent oral cancer; the loss of his father; serious auto accidents involving his sister Marsha, son Andrew, and son Nathan and his wife Amy; Carrie's diagnosis of metastatic pancreatic cancer in 2005; their son Matt's death, which was determined to be suicide, on May 5, 2007; Carrie's death just two months later on July 2, 2007. Stating unequivocally that "joy is completely independent of all the chances and changes of life," Gary instructs us in how we can cultivate sovereign joy in the midst of the winter season of life:

1) Set your mind on things above.

2) Choose to count your blessings and be faithful.

3) Choose to claim God's promises; they are so much more powerful than Satan's pessimism.

4) Choose to obey and act on what you know to be true.

5) Choose to invest in healthy relationships: God, family, friends.

Gary has chosen to offer the sacrifice of praise to God in the midst of what must seem like an interminable winter season in his life. He lives the life he teaches and preaches about, because he trusts in the One who is sovereign. His joy is not dependent on circumstances, but on the certainty of God's character.

I have come to cherish the words of the apostle Peter in his first letter, chapter 4:12-13, "Dear friends, do not be surprised at the painful trial you are suffering, as though something strange were happening to you. But rejoice that you participate in the sufferings of Christ, so that you may be overjoyed when His glory is revealed." One day, perhaps very soon, we will share in His glory. And until then, we choose to rejoice.

> **Faithful Father God**, it is by the most gracious gift of your Son, Jesus Christ, that we are redeemed and can be used in your service. Help us to be holy as you are holy, Lord, that we might daily present our bodies to you as living sacrifices for the glory of your Kingdom. In Jesus' name, Amen.

In the same way, the Spirit helps us in our weakness. We do not know what we ought to pray, but the Spirit Himself intercedes for us with groans that words cannot express. And He who searches our hearts knows the mind of the Spirit, because the Spirit intercedes for the saints in accordance with God's will. —Romans 8:26-27

23
Prayer

My earliest recollections of prayer were tidbits from early childhood. "Now I lay me down to sleep;" "God bless Mom and Dad, Tim, me, Jennifer and Mark, Grandma and Grandpa, all of our cousins, aunts and uncles" (we didn't have dogs or cats, or I'm sure they would have made the never-varying list, but apparently I didn't feel that turtles or fish merited inclusion); "Lord, forgive me for calling Mrs. Priest (my third-grade teacher) a pain in the neck;" all the prayers of a child, offered because I knew it was what good Christians did.

Then there were the prayers of my minister father, which seemed at the time tantamount to the epic novels of Tolstoy or Dostoevski, the duration of which was always commensurate with the magnitude of the meal being served. Thanksgiving guaranteed a table grace that would reward the wayward and disobedient furtive glances of the younger set with the clotting of Dad's own famous brown gravy as it congealed in the china boat. Christmas dinner at Grandma and Grandpa's was the War and Peace-length prayer event of the year, or so it seemed, as we antsy children struggled to "endure" the sumptuous meal that only served in our minds to delay the real intent and purpose of our day: PRESENTS!

As humbled as I am by the veracity of the preceding accounts, I must further confess that quite a bit more of life passed me by before I truly grasped the enormity of prayer and the gift that God gave to each of His children in offering us an intimate, conversational relationship with Him at any time and place. The impertinent, rolled eyes of my childhood and young adult years gave way to genuine awe and reverence as I began to see God meet me at whatever level I approached Him, speaking to me through His Word, other believers, life circumstances, and that still, small voice of His Spirit. One of my final gifts to Dad before he died was to tell him how much I missed his prayers and that I only wished they were that much longer!

CARRIE

Journal entry, October 12, 2005: Prayer. It is a phenomenal experience, gift, command, privilege, etc. This prayer pager I wear gives me hope—a sense that I am loved—and I am greatly encouraged that people are talking to Jesus. That is what it is ultimately about: a conversation with God and a belief that He hears us. So simple, yet so powerful.

Yes, it is so simple—and the most powerful tool we have in this life on earth: a personal, living relationship with God. He has allowed us to approach Him directly through the atoning blood of Jesus, which has cleansed us and enables us to stand in His presence washed clean of all sin. We know from Romans 8:34 that Jesus is at the right hand of God, making intercession for us: our Advocate pleading our case before the Most High. The question is, how do we get there? And why do we want to even go there?

All that I have learned about prayer is a result of my utter inability to deal with the vicissitudes of life on my own—in other words, out of sheer need. Hebrews 4:15-16 says it better than I can express:

> For we do not have a high priest who is unable to
> sympathize with our weaknesses, but we have one who

has been tempted in every way, just as we are—yet was without sin. Let us then approach the throne of grace with confidence, so that we may receive mercy and find grace to help us in our time of need.

My first grown-up attempts at prayer were cries for God's mercy and rescue through the pain of my early divorce. He did not remove me from the consequences of my own sin, but He did carry me through and help me to change as a result of it. He kept the promise that is recorded in James 4:8, "Draw near to God, and He will draw near to you." I felt safe in His presence, and trusted in the ways in which He was leading me.

When I met Philippe at Cherry Creek Presbyterian Church and we began "not dating," as he maintains—just becoming best friends—it was clear to me that this relationship, regardless of its ultimate outcome, needed to be founded on prayer. God had taught me a lesson! We began praying at the start and close of whatever it was we were doing together, inviting God to be Lord over us and to guide our thoughts and actions. Our friendship blossomed into a marriage that is still based on this practice. We can't imagine living without it.

We have, obviously, been severely tested during the twenty years of seeking the Lord as a couple, and can safely say that God always hears and answers prayer. The caveat is that it is not always in the way we think or hope it might be. Skeptics might argue that God will have His own way ultimately, so why bother praying? My answer is that it is not for the result; it is for the relationship. Yes, I would love to have my own way all of the time, but the Lord has given me a perspective on this that has indisputable evidence in my own life. The Father knows best!

We can quote Scripture until the cows come home, justifying God's seeming silence or even denial of a legitimate request, just like the friends of Job did. But when one is in the throes of cancer, the death of a spouse or child, the horror of disfigurement, the anguish of mental illness, the agony of divorce, the tortures of war, ad infinitum, all that seems like spiritual pablum. I have been in many of these circumstances and have generally found that the acute stage is not when I want well-meaning Christians to quote me pat verses. I'm sure I have been guilty of that very thing, as so often we don't know what to do or say when tragedy strikes. This is when the relationship we have developed with God takes over. If we have learned to trust Jesus' words in John 10:27, "My sheep listen to my voice; I know them, and they follow me. I give them eternal life, and they shall never perish; no one can snatch them out of my hand," then we can allow that same truth to sustain us for the duration of the trial. We have a history of His faithfulness.

My relationship with Carrie began with prayer before we even met. Not only had I begun praying for her because she was a friend of my friend Barb, I had also prayed with her over the phone the night before we met for the first time in the pre-op area at M.D. Anderson. Our hearts were so mutually attuned to our heavenly Father, with prayer as our lifeline, that calling on the Lord together was as natural as breathing. There was never any awkwardness or hesitancy; we simply joined hands, closed our eyes, and went before the One who would always listen—and answer.

God does not want to be seen as a remote figurehead who is ominous and inaccessible, but neither is He a Santa Claus who delivers endless bounty at our beck and call. He tells us in Revelation 3:20, "Here I am! I stand at the door and knock. If anyone hears my voice and opens the door, I will come in and eat with him, and he with me." The Creator, Sustainer, and Savior of the universe, just waiting for me to open the door! I don't even have to knock; He is the one who is relentlessly pursuing me! And if I ask, He will not withhold any good thing from me. The key is that He knows what is good, and I just think I do; His thoughts are not my thoughts; my ways are not His ways (Isaiah 55:8). It is just not all about me.

> As the heavens are higher than the earth, so are my
> ways higher than your ways and my thoughts than your

thoughts. As the rain and the snow come down from heaven, and do not return to it without watering the earth and making it bud and flourish, so that it yields seed for the sower and bread for the eater, so is my word that goes out from my mouth: It will not return to me empty, but will accomplish what I desire and achieve the purpose for which I sent it. You will go out in joy and be led forth in peace; the mountains and hills will burst into song before you, and all the trees of the field will clap their hands. Instead of the thornbush will grow the juniper, and instead of briers the myrtle will grow. This will be for the LORD's renown, for an everlasting sign, that will endure forever (Isaiah 55:9-13).

We labor for the imperishable, the incorruptible—not for the things that will pass away. Sometimes that looks like unanswered prayer, or even worse, denial of what we can only see as our heart's desire. We only understand in part, just as Paul says in I Corinthians 13, but one day we will see face to face. I am learning that it is a gift to be able to trust in God's heart when I can't begin to comprehend His ways; that this is how the Holy Spirit comforts me as He intercedes with those sighs that are too soft for words. I feel His presence, even if I don't understand how He works. I hate the thorn bushes and briers, the gut-wrenching pain of loss, as much as the next person. But "I know whom I have believed, and am convinced that He is able to guard what I have entrusted to Him for that day" (II Timothy 1:12).

I once interpreted "that day" only as the day I would greet my Savior and Lord face to face: the day of my death. I now wonder if it means something more: that Jesus Christ is able to guard ME—that which I have entrusted to Him, my body, mind and spirit—even for that day when my belief might be so challenged that I am tempted to fall away. Just as Jesus withstood the three temptations of the devil in the desert by knowing His Father and trusting Him so intimately, so can I—and all who believe in Him—trust the One in whom we believe, regardless of how He answers.

CARRIE

Journal entry, October 12, 2005: As I continue this journey, I still have to keep my heart and my eyes focused on God's love for me, His care for me, and His sovereignty. But I have learned some things from Scripture: I have learned that I can really bother Him with my pleas, I can tell Him of my desires, and I can "cry out to Him"—wail, if I want to. These are prayers and scriptures I pray and focus my heart upon as well as prayers of thanksgiving for who the Lord is in my life and how He remains at work to mold me, to change me, and to use me until my last breath—whenever that will be. Until that time, whether it is soon or in many years, I thank you for your prayers.

Precious Lord, there is no better place than near to your heart in prayer! Thank you that we can draw near to you with the assurance that you meet us wherever we are and take us where you want us to go. We know that you are achieving in us an eternal glory that outweighs the trials of this world. We trust you, Lord, and pray this in Jesus' name, Amen.

Dear friends, do not be surprised at the painful trial you are suffering, as though something strange were happening to you. But rejoice that you participate in the sufferings of Christ, so that you may be overjoyed when His glory is revealed. —I Peter 4:12

24

Suffering

Pain is a problem. One of the most frequently-posed questions of unbelievers to those who profess faith is undoubtedly, "How could a loving God allow such suffering in the world?" There is not a pat response to this, but a life lived for Christ will eventually reveal the answer. It is not one that is readily understood or embraced, but those who have suffered and persevered as Christians begin to see that our lives are indeed not our own; just as Christ gave His life so that we might live, so we participate in the sufferings of Christ so that we might also share in His glory.

I am mentally cataloging my encounters with pain as I struggle to formulate an adequate explanation for my own belief: that it is the very thing we most dread that will shape and refine us into that which God can use. The first significant physical pain I ever experienced was probably the brown recluse spider bite during my second year of college. Not able to put weight on my right leg, I languished in the hospital for eleven days before the Lord brought healing to my wound; I then hobbled around on crutches for some time after my release from the hospital. Some three- plus decades later, it seems virtually insignificant. My body has expunged the memory of that pain as completely as I can delete this sentence if I so choose (and I don't!). The next significant exposure came when I severely injured the nerves and tendons in my right arm in 1983. True to human nature, I thought it was the worst pain I could experience, as it was relentless and lasted two entire years. However, when it was divinely healed by God's hand in 1985, all I could remember was how gracious my heavenly Father had been to hear my prayers, as well as those of many others, and restore me.

Fast forward several years to 1990, and the word "pain" takes on new dimensions altogether. Two surgeries five weeks apart, one of them major, with the diagnosis of cancer, coupled with the grief over the loss of my unborn children and the subsequent removal of my entire reproductive system—now that qualifies as pain! The physical and emotional were so inextricably intertwined that I didn't know which was more intense. In a bizarre way, the consuming physical pain was almost my friend because it afforded a temporary distraction from my profound emotional losses, and provided an acceptable excuse for me to retreat from the world for a time. Still, as I reflect on that suffering from the vantage point of nineteen years more of life, I am filled with a poignant sweetness as I remember the struggle to trust God in the midst of the trial; His provision of such a loving husband, family, friends, and church; the times I was compelled to seek Him in ways beyond that which I had previously experienced; the power of the Holy Spirit to comfort in ways that surpassed human comprehension; the layers of maturity as God proved to me His promise to "work all things together for good for those who love Him and are called according to His purpose" (Romans 8:28).

After my initial cancer diagnosis and treatment, opportunities to grow through suffering didn't diminish…they increased with a good degree of rapidity! Apparently my visceral organs had been a bit rearranged during the surgery, so a couple of years later, I had my next date with pain. The culprit was my appendix, which had somehow found its way to the rear, so what had been thought to be a back problem resulted in an appendectomy. By this time, it was really no big deal, and I sailed through and was out shoveling snow (still in Denver, not Houston, mind you!) a week later. I was pretty proud of myself.

The true test came the day after Easter in 1996. I was assaulted by a sudden wave of pain that forced me to the floor. On admission to the hospital, no plausible explanation could be found for the unrelenting, writhing pain in my abdomen. Test after test revealed no abnormalities, and morphine combined with Demerol hardly made a dent in the pain. I have never spent such an interminable night as that one, alone in my hospital bed watching the second hand make its way around the face of the clock time after time after time. The pain was so all-encompassing that I simply trusted in the prayers of others as they interceded on my behalf rather than trying to talk to God myself. I do remember knowing that He was with me.

The next afternoon, my white cell count jumped from normal to twenty thousand, and a surgeon came in and said, "We're operating right away!" When they discovered a gangrenous intestine and diffuse peritonitis throughout the abdominal cavity, I understood why I had been in pain. Thirteen years later, I see this event as the moment when God redefined my sense of purpose in life and taught me that He wanted me to allow Him to use me for whatever He called me to do. And there is no memory of the pain.

Oswald Chambers has the pithy ability to zero in on the heart of a matter in a way that endears him to many and probably alienates many others. Being a great proponent of his teaching, I love to share excerpts from *My Utmost for His Highest* that summarize my own thoughts on suffering:

> To choose to suffer means that there is something wrong; to choose God's will even if it means suffering is a very different thing. No healthy saint ever chooses suffering; he chooses God's will, as Jesus did, whether it means suffering or not....God puts His saints where

they will glorify Him, and we are no judges at all of where that is.[26]

There is no such thing as a private life—"a world within the world"—for a man or woman who is brought into fellowship with Jesus Christ's sufferings. God breaks up the private life of His saints, and makes it a thoroughfare for the world on the one hand and for Himself on the other. No human being can stand that unless he is identified with Jesus Christ....Why shouldn't we go through heartbreaks? Through those doorways God is opening up ways of fellowship with His Son. Most of us fall and collapse at the first grip of pain; we sit down on the threshold of God's purpose and die away of self-pity, and all so-called Christian sympathy will aid us to our death bed. But God will not. He comes with the grip of the pierced hand of his Son, and says, "Enter into fellowship with Me; arise and shine." If through a broken heart God can bring His purposes to pass in the world, then thank Him for breaking your heart.[27]

It all sounds pretty severe, doesn't it? And yet, I have to say from what I have experienced that it is true. If Oswald Chambers isn't your spiritual cup of tea, then try A.W. Tozer:

There are people within the ranks of Christianity who have been taught and who believe that Christ will shield His followers from wounds of every kind. If the truth were known, the saints of God in every age were only effective after they had been wounded. They experienced the humbling wounds that brought contrition, compassion and a yearning for the knowledge of God.[28]

And now back to dear Oswald:

An average view of the Christian life is that it means deliverance from trouble. It is deliverance IN trouble, which is very different...God does not give us over-coming life: He gives us life as we overcome. The strain is the strength...The temptation is to face difficulties from a common-sense standpoint. The saint is hilarious when he is crushed with difficulties because the thing is so ludicrously impossible to anyone but God.[29]

The word "hilarious" may be just a bit over the top; perhaps I would say "exhilarated" instead.

One of Carrie's most beloved Bible passages was Psalm 91. Gary and I were actually discussing that on the phone as we were continuing to remember and grieve his precious wife and my dear friend a year after her death. How can we understand this psalm that so many have prayed over and over for protection in view of Carrie's death—or that of any other believer, for that matter? Again, I gained insight from Chambers. Quoting from the opening of Psalm 91, he writes, "'He that dwelleth in the secret place of the Most High...THERE shall no evil befall thee'—no plague can come nigh the place where you are at one with God."[30] In the words of Martin Luther, the same words that the Holy Spirit reminded me of as I lay on the gurney in pre-op before my hysterectomy on May 23, 1990, "This body they may kill; God's truth abideth still: His Kingdom is forever" (from "A Mighty Fortress is our God").

CARRIE

Journal entry, February 19, 2006: I was thinking of my life path on Valentine's Day, sitting on my bed getting treatment in Houston. I was listening to a song called "Untitled Hymn: Come to Jesus" by Chris Rice on my iPod and thought I would carve out what God has done and is doing, walking through the verses of this song.[31] Come along with me as I come to Jesus, sing to Jesus, cry out to Jesus, dance for Jesus, LIVE for Jesus!

I came to know Jesus as a student at the University of Nebraska. I will never forget the experience of understanding for the first time what Jesus did for me on the cross, and that I could walk with Him for the rest of my life. It transformed my heart instantly. I wanted, desired, craved His love and His

Word and fellowship with other believers. I craved "true" life. I could not get enough of His ability to heal my heart; my wrong choices. I still love singing to Him today when I feel His forgiveness and His grace. Just the fact that we are humans living on earth and are in relationships means that we will fall, and fall I have. I have made so many mistakes as a wife, a mother, and a friend. I have disappointed Jesus countless times, but love that I can "fall" into His arms or at His feet. As long as I am human and on this earth, I will continue to fall, but hope to fall into Him more and more.

Yes, crying is a major experience in my life. Cannot think of a day in the last year that at least my eyes have not welled up with tears. Since the cancer, crying almost always brings me Jesus in ways I had not experienced before this cancer.

I LOVE to dance! So many dancing times in my life: Christmas mornings as a little girl, my college days, moments with good friends, my wedding day, the birth of each child, the wedding of Nathan and Amy, etc. As I write this journal entry, I have had a 'dancing' week! Oh, so much to dance and rejoice over! I am getting fat! I have gone form 100 pounds to between 112 and 115! My digestive system is working better. My energy is up and I am walking and lifting weights for the first time since June. I am dancing over friendship and love and family and the love and healing grace of my Jesus. Dancing, dancing, dancing! I do feel alive!

Death: hearing this verse could be scary, especially having a disease that screams, "This experience is not far off!" But look at these words! They are power-packed with joy, and hope and fun and goodness and all that eternity has to offer with Jesus. Ever planned your funeral? I had done that even before this disease, so I know if I have done it, and I am not that unique, you have, too!

My funeral, whether it is next week or in forty years, will be filled with joy and singing and some laughter and a whole lot of hope. Imagine it for a few moments, and let yourself feel sweet eternal life. Each chorus of this lovely song calls us to Jesus, and in that experience, we find "life." I read this quote by Rick Warren this past week and feel the truth of it profoundly:

"God wants us to practice on earth what we will do forever in

eternity. We were made by God, and for God, and until we figure that out, life isn't going to make sense."

This same Chris Rice song had an equally powerful impact on my life and heart as well. I remember hearing Damaris Carbaugh's chocolatey-rich alto voice singing this on KHCB, my favorite Christian radio station, and just wanted to soak in it. As self-described "twins," Carrie and I loved this song, and every time I listen to it even now, I am blessed with memories of my dear friend.

The Friday before Carrie died, June 29, 2007, she and Gary called Philippe and me, asking us to intercede for them as she was hospitalized in Northwest Arkansas and her physical strength began to ebb away. As we prayed, I felt the Lord impress on me that I was to be a "watchman" that night, just standing in the gap and worshiping the Lord. What felt curious to me at the time was that the spirit of travail left me and I was overcome with the joy of the Lord! Immersing myself in music of praise, I sang and cried out and danced to Jesus with all that was within me. He inhabited my praises and filled me with the assurance that He was in control—of everything. The following day at noon, Carrie phoned me and we shared the last conversation we would have on earth.

Carrie had it figured out. I attended her memorial service on July 6, 2007, and everything that she had written came to pass: it was "filled with joy and singing and some laughter and a whole lot of hope." God was glorified in her life. He was glorified in her death, and now He continues to be glorified through the legacy that she has left. The words of Romans 5:2-5 come to mind:

> And we rejoice in the hope of the glory of God. Not only so, but we also rejoice in our sufferings, because we know that suffering produces perseverance; perseverance, character; and character, hope. And hope does not disappoint us, because God has poured out His love into our hearts by the Holy Spirit, whom He has given us.

Our loving heavenly Father, we know that in this world, we will have trials and pain, but we rejoice in the knowledge that you have overcome the world through the death and resurrection of your Son, our Lord and Savior. We await with hope your promise that we will one day be with you where there is no more death or mourning or crying or pain. We thank you that you are with us now and forever, and pray this in Jesus' name, Amen.

The Lord your God is with you, He is mighty to save. He will take great delight in you, He will quiet you with His love, He will rejoice over you with singing. —Zephaniah 3:17

25

Music

One of my most precious memories of our son's infancy is of my dad cradling his beloved little grandson Paul in the rocking chair of his sun-dappled nursery and ever so gently singing, "A sunbeam, a sunbeam; Jesus wants me for a sunbeam! A sunbeam, a sunbeam—I'll be a sunbeam for Him!" It was such a perfect metaphor of the scripture from Zephaniah: our loving heavenly Father delighting in each one of us, quieting us with His love, rejoicing over us with singing!

As one who was and is drawn to music like a magnet, I have early recollections of making myself a nuisance whenever we would visit friends or relatives who had a piano. I would eyeball everyone's living room to see if they were so endowed, and if they were, make my request known in no uncertain terms. Observing my compulsion which they sensed as a call, my dear parents sacrificed considerably to buy me a brand new piano and find the best piano teacher available, Mrs. Geraldine Grady. I took to it with a consuming passion and knew that I had found my purpose in life. What I didn't know was that God would allow me to go full-circle before I truly understood that all of the glory belonged to Him.

Many years ago, my mom needle-pointed for me a quotation from Martin Luther: "Music is a Fair and Glorious Gift of God." When I did a search for that on my computer, I was rewarded with further elaboration:

> I wish to see all arts, principally music, in the service of Him who gave and created them. I would not for all the world forego my humble share of music. Singers are never sorrowful, but are merry, and smile through their troubles in song. Music makes people kinder, gentler, more staid and reasonable. I am strongly persuaded that after theology, there is no art that can be placed on a level with music, for besides theology, music is the only art capable of affording peace and joy of the heart.

First as a student, then as a young professional musician, and now as a seasoned professor of music, I have experienced the gamut of this fair and glorious art, becoming all too aware that the temptation is to glorify the recipient rather than the Giver of the gift. Perhaps when one must practice for the better part of every day to hone the requisite skills, there is a tendency to appropriate a sense of ownership rather than one of stewardship. The only genuine satisfaction I have ever experienced in this realm is when I yield my talent to God and allow Him to receive all of the glory.

Music also served as my "cover-up" when I had to deal with unfamiliar or threatening emotions. Instead of taking my fears, relational wounds, or life dilemmas to the Lord in prayer, I pounded them out on the piano. It may have been temporarily cathartic, but left a whole lot of unfinished business. What comes to mind is when my brief first marriage was crumbling and I went down to the piano in the middle of the night and played Chopin's "Funeral March" sonata. Not too subtle, that!

Our God is always faithful, and He led me back to the shelter under His wing. For quite some time, I was unable to sing a hymn or praise song in church without tears pouring down my face. I now consider that a good thing—a God thing! The power of the Holy Spirit to gently convict us of our sin and wash us with the cleansing blood of Jesus is the only true healing and restoration. More than two decades later, my dear Philippe never leaves for church without tissues in his pocket for me!

My daily walk with God—the 24/7 kind of walk—always involves music. Colossians 3:16 is an apt description: "Let the word of Christ dwell in you richly as you teach and admonish one another with all wisdom, and as you sing psalms, hymns and spiritual songs with gratitude in your heart to God." Our home is filled with the sound of music, from Paul's contemporary Christian radio station to Philippe's worship CDs to my singing and playing.

One evening when Carrie was staying with us during her treatments at M.D. Anderson, she asked me to play the piano for her. I asked her whether she'd rather hear an arrangement of a praise song or a fugue from a Bach toccata I was learning. She opted for the Bach, being that he wrote everything to the glory of God, anyhow. When I finished playing, I was only aware of how dissatisfied I was with my performance, despite her very positive response. She said to me, "Jan, just how long do you think it will be before you're satisfied with this?" (That was my clinical therapist-twin-friend speaking!) I answered, "Probably never." That really got me thinking…that pesky perfectionism had reared its ugly head again! Even when I thought I was doing something "as unto the Lord," I was passing judgment on what I felt was lacking! Effectively, I was dissatisfied with what God had blessed me with for His use, to His glory. It didn't belong to me; I was only the steward. It was given to me to give away for Him.

Perhaps somewhere along the way, I had misinterpreted the words of Jesus in Matthew 5:48, "Be perfect, therefore, as your heavenly Father is perfect," and Paul's words in I Corinthians 10:31, "…whatever you do, do it all for the glory of God." My perfectionism was self-serving, not God-revering. I began to see that it was still infiltrating other areas of my life: my cooking, housekeeping, personal appearance (hated it when anybody would see me "unmade")—even prayer! My dear friend Carrie had spoken one pivotal sentence, phrased as a question, delivered with love, just as we are told to do in Ephesians 4:15, "Speaking the truth in love, we will in all things grow up into Him who is the Head; that is, Christ."

Carrie's admonishment became an exhortation to me as I allowed the Lord to teach me what I needed in order to grow up into Him. Having had a lifelong inhibition about singing in public, despite the fact that it is my profession to train singers, I began to sense the Lord urging me to yield this area to Him as well. At first, I protested, "But Lord—you know I can't sing one line of a hymn without crying!" And His tacit answer was, "Let the tears flow." Gradually, I have begun allowing Him to inhabit my praises in this way. Last night, as I was ministering through prayer at the bedside of a man who had experienced a paralyzing stroke and then brain surgery, the Spirit moved in him and he whispered "Hallelujah." The same Spirit moved in me, and I began singing, "Hallelujah, hallelujah, hallelujah…" Then this precious man, with his weak and raspy post-operative voice gaining strength in the Lord, called out, "Glory to the Lamb!" I began to sing, "Glory, glory, GLORY to the LAMB! For the Lord is great, and worthy of all praise; the Lamb upon His throne!" Tears were streaming down my face as I gloried in the Lord: His power to heal, to overcome, to inhabit our praises!

The "Hallelujah Chorus" from Handel's *Messiah* is arguably the most beloved and oft-performed choral work of all time. Based on three passages from the book of Revelation, the majesty of the music suitably frames the word of God:

> Hallelujah! For the Lord God Omnipotent reigneth.
> The kingdom of this world is become the Kingdom
> of our Lord and of His Christ; and He shall reign for
> ever and ever. King of kings, and Lord of lords, and
> He shall reign forever and ever. Hallelujah!

At the first London performance of *Messiah* during the reign of King George II, legend has it that the king stood during the Hallelujah chorus and that everyone in the audience then observed protocol and stood with him, resulting in the long-standing (yes, a pun) tradition that we observe to this day. But why did the king stand? I prefer to think that the glory of the Lord could not be contained and that he simply had to rise to his feet in worship, acknowledging Christ the Messiah as the King of all kings and the Lord of all lords. This earthly king humbled himself that Christ the King might be exalted.

It has been so liberating to admit that I'm not perfect, never have been, and don't need to be...at least, not as the world sees "perfect." I want to be perfect as my heavenly Father is perfect: perfect in love—His love. My aspiration is to glorify and enjoy God and to grasp how wide and long and high and deep that love is, to know that love which surpasses knowledge—so that I may one day be filled to the measure of all the fullness of God. Now that's perfect! Hallelujah!

> **Our gracious heavenly Father**, my heart is singing "Hallelujah" to you right now as I praise you for the gift of music and the joy of sharing it with the world. May your name always be glorified as we sing songs, hymns and spiritual songs with one another in the name of Jesus. It is in His name we pray, Amen.

These were all commended for their faith, yet none of them received what had been promised. God had planned something better for us so that only together with us would they be made perfect. —Hebrews 11:39

26

Healing

"It's a bird…it's a plane…it's…………….Superman!!!" Funny how tidbits from the remote past can be evoked by the juxtaposition of two vultures scavenging for breakfast at about one hundred feet in the air while a jetliner completed the triangle in my field of vision at about three hundred times that altitude. If I didn't understand any of the laws of physics governing time and space, I might think that they were all the same size, and that the birds were flying faster than the plane. I've often thought it curious that I can get on a Boeing 777 at Houston Intercontinental and fly to Tokyo, Japan in less time than it would take me to drive to my childhood home in Chicago, Illinois.

What on earth—or in heaven, for that matter—does this have to do with healing? The answer I have found is that I do not see life from God's vantage point. He sees everything from the fullness of eternity, with no boundaries to time and space, and I see my own little life as if the world revolves around it. I judge His actions and responses to my prayers based on my needs as I see them today, without any true comprehension of the eternal implications. I know and trust that He is able to speak healing to my body, mind and spirit, but sometimes it seems as though He chooses to withhold the very thing that I so fervently request. I have wrestled like Jacob and questioned like Job; I have wandered like Jonah and wept like Jeremiah. But I keep coming back to Jesus, the Alpha and the Omega, the Beginning and the End.

CARRIE

Journal entry, January 6, 2007: Ever since the diagnosis of this disease, I have been listening to the Lord, reading His word and incorporating His truth into my life. One challenge I believe we all face is our theology of God's work in our lives concerning "healing." From the beginning of the diagnosis, I have been prayed over for healing and people continue to pray for healing for my body—complete and total healing of the disease. Many prayer intercessors have said from the beginning that I would be going on a journey and that healing would not be immediate, but that I would experience healing. Much of my reading, secular books included, encourages people with disease to not focus on the symptoms, but to keep looking beyond symptoms to the "possibility of the impossible." All have said that fear is crippling, is disease-producing, and accomplishes nothing.

I love the stories from the Bible where people simply came to Jesus with faith that a look from Him, a touch of His robe, a few soft words would relieve them of their pain or restore their health. These stories are with me every day. I have learned that God "hates" disease as He hates sin. He does not strike us with disease, and is grieved over our pain and sorrow. I have learned that fighting disease and seeking healing is a battle between dark and light, and the mind is constantly being pulled in the direction of the earth as opposed (to being pulled) towards heaven. I have come to love the Lord's prayer, "Thy Kingdom come, Thy will be done on earth as it is in heaven." We can have heaven on this earth, and heaven on this earth is a part of God's will as it is manifested through His power.

Speaking from the perspective of one who has been committed to fervent prayer and intercession over a period of many years, I know that God does heal and does manifest His power on earth as it is in heaven; I have experienced it several times myself and witnessed it in others. The healing that lasts, however, is that which results from God's transformation of our temporal perspective into the scope of His time and place. One who knew the life-altering power of God perhaps as well as any was the apostle Paul, who says in Romans 12:1-2:

> Therefore, I urge you, brothers, in view of God's mercy, to offer your bodies as living sacrifices, holy and pleasing to God—which is your spiritual worship. Do not conform any longer to the pattern of this world, but be transformed by the renewing of your mind. Then you will be able to test and approve what God's will is—His good, pleasing and perfect will.

My most recent struggle with this physical body also presented a spiritual conundrum. I had been miraculously healed of the two herniated disks in my cervical spine four years ago after years of chronic and often debilitating pain. Although I had prayed and been prayed over more times than I could count, I was not healed —but one day, I woke up completely without pain! God had released His power and removed my distress. However, beginning nearly two years ago, I developed two new herniations in my lumbar spine, causing increased numbness and difficulty in walking. The distress became very disabling, but I didn't sense the permission of the Lord to seek surgical intervention, although I was under a doctor's care. Well-meaning friends would recommend surgeons, but I kept answering, "I don't sense that God is taking me there; I want to wait on Him and see what He will do. What He has done before, He is able to do again."

The symptoms mounted and we upped the fervor of our prayers. Philippe and I were both trusting in God to manifest Himself in a miraculous way. On Tuesday, May 6, 2008, I could hardly sit, stand, or lie down, much less walk. My dear friend and prayer partner, Sarah Purcell, called to find out how I was. As I shared my conviction that the Lord was able to heal me by His hand, she said, "Jan, just because you're in prayer and healing ministry doesn't always mean that God will choose to heal you." This truth resonated in me, I hung up the phone, and I called a very prominent neurosurgeon in the Houston Medical Center. I anticipated a wait time of six to eight weeks for an appointment, and was flabbergasted when his assistant called back and offered me a time two days later!

Meanwhile, I was prompted to call a prominent orthopedic spine surgeon the next day for another opinion, and was astonished when the nurse asked if I could come in the same day! I was so immediately convicted of this being God's answer to our prayers that I proceeded to schedule surgery for that Friday, May 9. The surgeon had planned to be out of town, but a minor auto accident that same morning would prevent his leaving, and he offered me the time. Wasn't that just like God?!

After much prayer, I decided to keep the appointment with the neurosurgeon, despite the already-scheduled surgery. This was to be a divine appointment, for I was able to minister in the doctor's waiting room to a man who was suffering from agonizing pain. In addition, the neurosurgeon confirmed the procedure that the orthopedic spinal surgeon planned to use.

On the morning of my surgery, there was a sudden whoosh of activity around the pre-surgical cubicle at eight a.m., and in came the entire team of doctors and nurses along with a precious friend from church, Lorrie Foster, who is a chaplain at that hospital. My surgeon, Dr. Ngu, took my right hand, my dear Philippe took my left hand, and the others formed a circle of seven as Lorrie led us in prayer. Tears were streaming from the corners of my eyes as I was immersed in the depths of God's protective love. I learned a few days later that another friend had prayed that every hand that touched me while I was in the hospital would be hand-picked by God. And they were!

God did not heal me in the way I had anticipated; He did not answer my prayers the same way He had the last time. He had a far greater perspective than I, and a purpose I couldn't possibly fathom. He wanted to touch many other lives in the process of healing me, He chose to do it in His way and time, and He was glorified.

CARRIE

Journal entry, January 6, 2007: There are camps of people that (maintain) that if God wants it done, He will do it, and if not, it won't happen. And that's that. I steer pretty clear of this thinking. When we approach healing and how God works in this black and white manner, we put Him in a box and diminish the complexity of all that God is. We make Him two-dimensional.

While God is a God of absolutes, He is not concrete or two-dimensional. He is one trillion-dimensional and more; I just don't know what comes after a trillion! When we approach God with this "box" theology, it would seem that there is no need to pray, to study His Word and proclaim, or to intercede for others if God is just going to do what He is going to do. Studying hope, the battle of the mind, my own sinful pride and fear, learning to pray and cry out to God for myself and for others are all things that I have grown in during this disease as I discover more about God and healing.

The awareness that Carrie and I became friends in January, 2006, a full eight months after her official cancer diagnosis in May, 2005, causes me to pause with a measure of incredulity at God's sovereign healing provision. She had only been expected, according to the medical statistics, to live for three to six months after diagnosis. Instead, she lived another two years and two months. Her passion for life increased immeasurably during that time; she did Kingdom work with a zeal that was simply astounding. Carrie became a lifelong friend to me, a Kingdom friend—first on earth, and then one day in heaven. God knew that I needed Carrie's unique imprint on my life and gradually showed both of us that He had a greater purpose for our friendship than what was immediately apparent to us on earth. Her impact continues now and forever, because she trusted in Christ and lived for things of eternal value. Carrie persevered in the greatest storm of her life, and found the Anchor that holds.

I simply love God's gracious gifts to us each day, revealed in big and little surprise packages. My first one this morning was in one of my devotionals for today, July 9, from the anthology *Tozer on the Holy Spirit*:

> We are in the midst of the storm of life. The believing saints of God are on board the ship. Someone looks to the horizon and warns, "We are directly in the path of the typhoon! We are as good as dead. We will surely be dashed to pieces on the rocks!" But calmly someone else advises, "Look down, look down! We have an anchor!" We look, but the depth is too great. We cannot see the anchor. But the anchor is there. It grips the immovable rock and holds fast. Thus the ship outrides the storm. The Holy Spirit has assured us that we have an Anchor, steadfast and sure, that keeps the soul....The Spirit is saying to us, "Keep on believing. Pursue holiness. Show diligence and hold full assurance of faith to the very end. Follow those who through faith and patience inherit what has been promised." He is faithful![32]

Tozer's words evoked those of William Bradbury in the second verse of his beloved hymn classic, "The Solid Rock:"

> When darkness veils His lovely face,
> I rest on His unchanging grace;
> In every high and stormy gale,
> my anchor holds within the veil.
> On Christ the solid Rock I stand
> all other ground is sinking sand.
> All other ground is sinking sand.

Most merciful Father, You are the Anchor of my soul; you are the Rock on which I stand. Through the raging storms of life, you are faithful and will lead your children safely to refuge. We put all of our trust in you, and pray this in Jesus' name, Amen.

So I will always remind you of these things, even though you know them and are firmly established in the truth you now have. I think it is right to refresh your memory as long as I live in the tent of this body, because I know that I will soon put it aside, as our Lord Jesus Christ has made clear to me. And I will make every effort to see that after my departure you will always be able to remember these things. —II Peter 1:12-15

27

Making Memories

CARRIE

Journal entry, October 15, 2006: I cannot adequately put into words what I have experienced regarding "memories" since the cancer diagnosis. I don't think that my experience with memories is original and do wonder if some of you have experienced the same phenomenon. I have memories and they are vivid and random. Usually my memories are triggered by something such as a backdrop, a movie, people interacting, smells, etc., and I am immediately taken back to a specific time of my life that I remember in detailed experience. I can't make these memories happen; they just happen with the triggers. I have thought of childhood experiences: playing in the tall grasses, making playhouses with rooms; climbing my favorite box elder tree; riding my horse, and the smell of him when I took the saddle off after a long, hard run; riding with my dad on the feed wagon; many Sundays spent water skiing and playing in the lake with friends and family.

I have vivid memories of my college days, living in the Delta Gamma house and often choosing the very end rooms, looking out the corner windows at "R" Street, daydreaming about what would happen next: class, a Nebraska football game, a sorority function.

I have thought of precious times with the boys and Gary, especially our times in Colorado. Just living in our house there, sitting on the couch in the evenings, reading stories to the boys. Other memories have come, too: certain camping trips and moments on those trips, smelling the smells of the mountains and remembering the beauty of the changing Aspen trees. Sometimes I remember moments with friends: a birthday celebration, or simply just sitting in their kitchen or living room, chatting. I remember trudging into Starbucks through the snow for a cup of coffee with a friend, feeling cozy once inside. A vivid memory I have is of the first few weeks after our move to Colorado. It was snowing on a Saturday and I went craft shopping with two friends. No one was bothered about driving in the snow and it was beautiful as it stuck to the pine trees. We ended our shopping with lunch at warm and wonderful Marie Callender's. That memory has never left me.

Most of my memories just pop into my head and they are of things I have not thought of in a long time; they feel like I am right there. The faces of the people I am with, the background, the time of day, the time of month and time of year, and how old I was. There is a show on TV that always reminds me of when I attended Denver Seminary. I didn't watch the show then, but many of the people I knew at seminary did, so it makes me think of these people and that time in my life.

Why do I talk of memories? When life becomes something you value—every breathing moment, because you are not suffering and have not died—memories are the links from our past to our present and we also understand they are the links from our present to our future, so I work hard now to "make memories." While I had just had chemotherapy before going to the Buffalo River and Ponca City with our Bible study friends, I would not have missed the trip for anything because I knew I would be making memories. The food we ate, watching the kids have great fun, the smell of the cabin fire, the laughter and silliness, the beauty of the hike that I actually took, even though my legs felt like spaghetti.

I made a recent memory with my son Andrew. We went on a mother-son date to the beautiful new outdoor Promenade Mall in Northwest Arkansas. We chose to eat at P.F. Chang's, sharing our favorite steamed dumplings appetizer. Andrew is my youngest son, soon to be seventeen. He has changed with how he deals with me since the cancer. He no longer is embarrassed to put his arm

around me and he hugs me every day more than once and tells me he loves me.
I think he is making memories. We sat at the table over dinner that evening
and we talked very candidly about what it means to have passion for Jesus, how
to make good choices, dating, my concern for him, his concern for me, and if I
should die, how would he survive. We left the restaurant, got coffee, and laughed
and shopped and enjoyed being together. He told me I looked cool that evening.
That is quite a compliment—and you'd better believe I will "remember" what
I had on so I can be cool more often! It was a "Perfect Memory."

Watching a video on creativity in the past two weeks, I learned a new
approach to life. There are different lenses to see life with. When I believe I can
change the lenses and gain a new perspective, a different way of seeing something,
I find this links directly to hope and peace and freedom. I am thankful that
I have a variety of lenses in my life through God's word, and as I change the
lenses, this cancer becomes different: less looming, more hopeful, and definitely
not as defeating. Making memories allows us to use our lenses in creative ways,
and when we look back, oh—how our hearts are full and enriched.

Being the task-oriented, goal-setting overachiever that I am
(or hopefully, was!), my own journey through cancer and the subsequent related surgeries brought a new awareness of the significance of making memories. I had put my nose to the grindstone
so assiduously in order to attain what I thought was important in
my life that I really didn't know how to stop and smell the roses.
One of the memories I hold dear of the first few weeks of our
marriage is of Philippe and me standing in the curtain rods aisle of
Home Depot. I just wanted to snatch whatever met the measure-
ment requirements of our windows, but he thought it prudent to
examine color, quality, price—you name it! Twenty minutes later,
all I could focus on was how we had wasted a third of an hour in
Home Depot! What I completely missed was that I was "wasting"
it with the person I loved most in the world!

So often as we move along in life, we remember and record
(or our mothers do!) all of the "firsts": first tooth, first step, first
word, first day of school—and then later on, our first kiss, first

car, first house, first child—and they become the markers of our journey. They just don't really tell the story. We have to put on those other lenses Carrie had learned about and see life in the way God has designed it for us.

Many of us begin the Christian walk with so much zeal, filled with the wonder of God's redeeming love through the shed blood of Christ and pledging to know and love and serve Him all of our days. Then life intrudes and those things that scream for immediate attention take precedence over our daily quiet time with the Lord. Since God does not force Himself on any of us, it is easy to rationalize our occasional lapses, but sooner or later, the distancing begins to erode that most essential relationship of all.

About a year after we moved from Denver to Houston, during the time I now refer to as my "wilderness experience," I was sitting in the breakfast room reading the paper early one morning before our three-year-old Paul awakened. Although I didn't hear an audible voice, the Holy Spirit kept whispering, "Seek ye first the Kingdom of God…," as I persisted in making my way through the Houston Chronicle. After several days of this routine, that still, small voice seemed to be increasing in volume! "But Lord, you know I'll get to my Bible eventually; this is MY time!" I protested. However, I couldn't ignore His prompting any longer, as I could no longer even concentrate on the newspaper. The next day, I picked up my Bible and have had breakfast with God virtually every day since. It is absolutely a glorious time that I look forward to every morning—and we eventually canceled the paper! No news is good news, right? And the Good News is the BEST news!

After Moses received the Ten Commandments from God, he summoned the Israelites and told them of the commands, decrees and laws that God directed him to teach them:

> These commandments that I give you today are to be upon your hearts. Impress them on your children. Talk about them when you sit at home and when you walk along the road, when you lie down and when you get

up. Tie them as symbols on your hands and bind them on your foreheads. Write them on the doorframes of your houses and on your gates (Deuteronomy 6:6-9).

He instructed God's people to make memories of Him with their children. We are to pass His Word and the testimonies of His faithfulness to every generation.

Philippe's family owns a magnificent old home on Lake Neuchatel in Switzerland that was once a monastery and dates back to the fourteenth century. Portraits of ancestors appear to assess your every move, and there is even a room devoted to the family archives. What Paul likes best, though, are the stories—particularly of his own dad growing up, playing, and getting into occasional mischief in that very same place. They have a shared history; a legacy. It doesn't matter in the least that Paul was adopted into the de Chambrier family; he is a rightful heir with all of the privileges of the others who were born into it.

In a like manner, we are co-heirs with Christ, adopted into the family of God with all the rights and privileges thereof:

For He chose us in Him before the creation of the world to be holy and blameless in His sight. In love He predestined us to be adopted as His sons through Jesus Christ, in accordance with His pleasure and will—to the praise of his glorious grace, which He has freely given us in the One He loves. In Him we have redemption through His blood, the forgiveness of sins, in accordance with the riches of God's grace that He lavished on us with all wisdom and understanding (Ephesians 1:4-8).

What better memory is there than that?

Carrie lived that memory and died that memory. She viewed life through the lenses of eternal perspective and knew that every encounter was precious, to be lived to the fullest and to the glory of God. In my writing of this book, I have had the opportunity to relive virtually every memory I have of Carrie. She comes to mind and heart countless times every day, sometimes in the most mundane aspects of life. I think of Carrie when I decide to wear something pink in the morning. I remember her when I pass Starbucks. I savor her memory right along with the tart-sweet crispness of our favorite apple, "Pink Lady." Her intrepid fortitude inspires me when I encounter fears and obstacles in my own life. Her love reminds me of what Jesus tells us in John 15:12, "Love one another as I have first loved you."

I asked Carrie's precious friend Cheryl Carmichael to summarize for me how Carrie viewed my relationship with her, partly for the sake of perspective for the benefit of the reader, but also because I so miss her and yearn to meld the past with the present. In an e-mail on April 27, 2009, Cheryl wrote:

> First of all, I believe you defined HOPE. You came into her life when she needed to see that there are those who come out on the other side of cancer and beat it here on earth. You were also PEACE. You had an inner peace that had been cultivated through much prayer and self-relinquishing. Her need for you, I believe, increased as she drew closer to you and truly saw the evidence of the Holy Spirit's work in your life. You were FAITH. It was and is amazing how she wanted to hear from you in her final moments here on earth. Your commitment to the Word of God brought comfort, peace and rest to her very weary mind, body and spirit that day.

Wow. That was exceedingly abundantly more than I could ask or even imagine. How gracious of God, working through Cheryl's memories, to bless me with such affirmation in the present so that this story of His perfect provision will continue to be shared in the future.

The very last time I saw Carrie was less than two weeks before she died, when she and Gary stayed with us during her routine appointments at M.D. Anderson. Shortly after their departure very early on Wednesday, June 20, 2007, Carrie phoned to say that she had left her contact lenses in our guest room and asked if I would put them in the mail. I packed them carefully, and because I remembered that Carrie loved cherry Jolly Ranchers (another trait we "twins" shared), I bought several bags of assorted flavors and sifted out all the cherry ones to send along with the lenses. I couldn't resist adding a little note: "Your contacts are keeping an eye on all those Jolly Ranchers!" My package arrived on the day Carrie walked into the presence of Jesus with perfect sight.

> **Precious Lord,** we are so grateful for the stories of your faithfulness recorded in the Bible and for the power of the testimonies of those who have gone before us. Thank you for creating us with the ability to remember so that we can teach our children what you have done. We give you the glory as we pray this in Jesus' name, Amen.

For you were once darkness, but now you are light in the Lord. Live as children of light (for the fruit of the light consists in all goodness, righteousness and truth) and find out what pleases the Lord. —II Corinthians 5:8-10

28

Transparency

I have a vague recollection from my elementary school art class of the differences between "opaque," "translucent," and "transparent." Opaque objects do not reflect light; those that are translucent allow light to pass through, but only in part; things that are transparent can be seen through. As a Christian adult, I see some very apt metaphors here!

"For Satan himself masquerades as an angel of light. It is not surprising, then, if his servants masquerade as servants of righteousness" (I Corinthians 11:14-15). Satan, the father of lies, the master deceiver, was called Lucifer: "light." But we who know the Truth also know that you can't get any more opaque than the devil! He rebelled against God and took a third of the angels of heaven along with him; now he "prowls around like a roaring lion, looking for someone to devour" (I Peter 5:8).

What about the "in-betweeners" of the world, the translucent? They subscribe to moral relativism, or perhaps feel that there are many paths to God. They don't yet really know that Jesus is "the way and the truth and the life"; that no one comes to the Father except through Him (John 14:6). The Word as recorded in Revelation

3:15-18 is pretty unequivocal:

> I know your deeds, that you are neither cold nor hot. I wish you were either one or the other! So, because you are lukewarm—neither hot nor cold—I am about to spit you out of my mouth. You say, "I am rich; I have acquired wealth and do not need a thing." But you do not realize that you are wretched, pitiful, poor, blind and naked. I counsel you to buy from me gold refined in the fire, so you can become rich; and white clothes to wear so you can cover your shameful nakedness; and salve to put on your eyes, so you can see.

Whew! To me, the choice is clear: transparency. I committed my life to Christ when I was sixteen years old, but I admittedly walked the "translucent" lifestyle for a while during my twenties and early thirties. As I think back over that time, I gradually allowed the powers of darkness to eclipse the light of Christ in me by not staying in the Word of God, not confessing my sins, and associating primarily with people who challenged and even refuted what I believed. I became spiritually blinded for a time, and this led to a non-biblical and disastrous first marriage and a significant detour from the path that God had prepared for me. It was grace, that of the blood of Jesus, that brought me back to His light.

Bob Sorge, the author of *Secrets of the Secret Place*, addresses this matter in the chapter entitled, "The Secret of Bodily Light." He quotes a passage from Luke 11: "The lamp of the body is the eye. Therefore, when your eye is good, your whole body also is full of light. But when your eye is bad, your body also is full of darkness." Sorge goes on to comment:

> It's fascinating that Jesus spoke of our bodies as though they can be filled with either light or darkness. The implications of this truth are vitally important to our victory and joy in Christ...There is a place in God where our bodies are full of light, where all darkness has been eradicated from our bodies. This is a place

of incredible freedom from temptation. Temptation often finds its power in the fact that it is able to appeal to dark areas within our body. When the body is full of light, bodily sins lose their power over us, and we walk in a fantastic dimension of victory.[33]

Since we are spiritual beings living in a temporal world, it is easy to forget at times that "our struggle is not against flesh and blood, but against the rulers, against the authorities, against the powers of this dark world and against the spiritual forces of evil in the heavenly realms" (Ephesians 6:12). However, He who is in us is greater than he who is in the world! (I John 4:4) God equips us with His armor, but we must also choose to resist the devil and walk in the light. I had a false sense of security as a college student that my faith was "banked" and could be withdrawn as if it were contained in an ATM! I learned about "overdrawal" the hard way!

In the first chapter of the book of James, verses 22-25, he writes:

> Do not merely listen to the Word, and so deceive yourselves. Do what it says. Anyone who listens to the Word but does not do what it says is like a man who looks at his face in a mirror and, after looking at himself, goes away and immediately forgets what he looks like. But the man who looks into the perfect law that gives freedom, and continues to do this, not forgetting what he has heard, but doing it—he will be blessed in what he does.

Mom was right—you are what you eat! Spiritual food, the Word of God, is to be digested so that it becomes part of who we are, "Christ in us, the hope of glory" (Colossians 1:27).

CARRIE

Journal entry, December 10, 2005: I just finished a book entitled The Importance of Being Foolish: How to Think Like Jesus *by Brennan*

Manning. The book's theme is our ability as humans to deceive ourselves, even to the point of our perspective of who Jesus is and his role in our lives. To best illustrate what God has spoken to my heart is to add here a few of the powerful quotes and words used by Manning:

> "The Lord said he wished me to be a fool, the like of which was never seen before," said Francis of Assisi. A gentle revolution will come through the little cadre of Christian fools who are willing to overthrow the established order by rearranging their lives around the mind of Christ. Their quest is transparency through truthfulness, and their lifestyles will be shaped by the gospel of Jesus Christ.[34]

> Self-deception is the enemy of wholeness because it prevents us from seeing ourselves as we really are. It covers up our lack of growth in the Spirit of the truthful One and keeps us from coming to terms with our real personalities.[35]

> To have the mind of Christ Jesus, to think His thoughts, share His ideals, dream His dreams, throb with His desires, replace our natural responses to persons and situations with the concern of Jesus, and make the mind-set of Christ so completely our own that "the life I now live in the body, I live by faith in the Son of God, who loved me and gave Himself for me" (Galatians 2:20), is not the secret of or the shortcut to transparency. It is transparency. Often our preoccupation with the three most basic human desires, pleasure, security and power, is the cloak that covers transparency. The endless struggle for enough money, good feelings, and prestige yields a rich harvest of worry, frustration, suspicion, anger, jealousy, anxiety, fear and resentment.[36]

> Here is the essence of perfect sincerity in conduct, to care for nothing but God's judgment on our actions, not to vary our attitude to suit the company we are in, not to hold one opinion when alone and adopt another in conversation, but to speak and act as in the sight of God who can read our inmost thoughts. (A Powerful Ending to the Book...)

When we are hungry for God, we move and act, become alive and responsive; when we are not, we are only playing spiritual games. "God is of no importance unless He is of supreme importance," said Abraham Heschel. An intense inner desire to learn to think like Jesus is already the sign of God's presence. The rest is the operation and activity of the Holy Spirit. I suppose most of us are in the same position as the Greeks who approached Philip and said, "We would like to see Jesus" (John 12:21). The only question is, "How badly?"[37]

As I travel this journey of cancer some would call terminal, I have had the choice to throw myself into the arms of Jesus or to run the other way, overtaken by fear, anxiety, perhaps anger at the idea that a loving God could allow such a disease in my life. I cannot, with all the strength in my voice and breath in my body, say how deeply grateful I am for the understanding that I must throw myself into the arms of Jesus, and when I do, that I become accountable in ways I never understood as seriously before this illness. My sin is real every day to me and I cannot carry it long before I take it to Him. I give Him my tears because I know that He is my loving Father who knows my pain anyway. I thank Him, thank Him, thank Him for His presence, His Word, and the truth of His Word that I am continuing to discover how to live out each day, and like a normal human, sometimes I fail. Transparency is not a complete uncovering with no boundaries of who we are, but rather it is agreeing with Jesus about who we are. We are people who fail, who are weak, who need Jesus and are made in God's image a little lower than the angels. Every day I embrace this truth, I embrace my Jesus.

Carrie truly helped me to become more transparent as I observed the freedom she had to share her struggles, not just with cancer, but with what human beings face every day we live in this world. I had become an expert at presenting the image I wanted everyone to see, regardless of whether or not it represented the truth. In the incisive words of my dear son Paul, I was a "poser." Carrie helped me to see that I didn't need to filter my feelings or reactions, or to shelter others from their own. I just needed to take ti :m directly to the One who could understand and help me to deal with them:

> This is the message we have heard from Him and declare to you: God is light; in Him there is no darkness at all. If we claim to have fellowship with Him yet walk in the darkness, we lie and do not live by the truth. But if we walk in the light, as He is in the light, we have fellowship with one another, and the blood of Jesus, His Son, purifies us from all sin. If we claim to be without sin, we deceive ourselves and the truth is not in us. If we confess our sins, He is faithful and just and will forgive us our sins and purify us from all unrighteousness (I John 1:5-10).

Gracious God, You have made us in your likeness and desire for us to be conformed to the image of your Son, Jesus Christ. Help us to so earnestly hunger for you and seek your face, Lord, that we would be continually filled with your light and the fullness of your glory. In Jesus' name, Amen.

But He lifted the needy out of their affliction and increased their families like flocks. —Psalm 107:41

29

Family

CARRIE

Journal entry, July 3, 2005: I thought about my family very frequently this week. Andrew came home from three weeks in Ireland, full of life and stories and godly experiences, plus he had just a whole heck of a lot of fun! Isn't that great—"fun"? Fun that did not involve the evils that Satan would convince him are fun, but just good, clean, godly fun with people from a different culture and the JBU community. Doesn't get much better than that. We said goodbye to Nathan and Amy after my chemo treatment on Friday, as they would be making their way to Florida and preparation for their wedding. Lots of tears, but prayers of joy. My heart cannot wait for this wedding! I miss them both. My dear parents (Marilyn and Vic Webster) arrived yesterday, July 2nd, to spend the 4th with us and to help out this weekend after chemo. My mom is the best mom in the world. I am forty-six and she is still all mom to her daughters. Her name from the grandchildren is Mimi. She is paying for a house cleaner for me to come once a month during my six months of chemo, and this is what moms do, especially ones whose own homes could win the Good Housekeeping Award of the Year for cleanliness. I love having her around and know that my cancer is hard on her heart. This is when distance is not a friend. I have two sisters, one of them a physician (Chris), as I have mentioned before. She is good to me and keeps up on both my physical and emotional walk. My little sister (Barb) is so tender, as is my dad, and in their quiet ways, I am sure that they have no idea why this is happening to me. Gary's sister Marsha is very much a sister to me as well, and as I walk my road, I have come a little bit closer to understanding her own journey of living life with pain. She has been such a model of someone who lives the gift of life to the fullest. All my family is very protective of me, wanting nothing to hurt me or make me sad. I see this especially with Matt and Gary. They are my protectors. They watch out for me, trying hard to keep me safe. I can't imagine walking through this cancer without family or without my Jesus.

I had trouble sleeping last night; the compressor on our just-repaired AC was laboring overtime in the muggy July heat, and I restlessly contemplated what I would write about today. I arose about three a.m. and noticed that Paul was still upstairs. After re-monstrating him for the umpteenth-gazillion time for playing video games in the middle of the night, he said, "Since neither of us can sleep, wanna come to my room and talk?" I left my grumpiness upstairs and cuddled up with him and our teensy Italian greyhounds, Max and Ali. We joked and laughed uproariously for over an hour, and I told Paul how thankful I am for him as my son.

I have been immeasurably blessed by my family, this closely-knit circle of three (really five, counting the dogs!). Philippe and Paul are my perennial cheerleaders, my gift-givers, my spiritual, emotional, and physical support through thick and thin. They think I'm great when I know I'm not!

I have also been blessed by my family of origin. I was the second child of four—Tim, Jan, Jennifer and Mark. Although we had perhaps more than our share of trials, my parents were godly Christians and raised us in the nurture and admonition of the Lord. I have often relished the sweet memories of my growing-up years with my family: the road trips to my mom's childhood home on the farm in Ransom, Illinois; visits to our dear Herbert grandparents in Chicago; vacations to northern Minnesota, Wisconsin, Washington, D.C., Colorado. During these times, we often sang together, especially with my dad and mom harmonizing on gospel hymns. Then there were the impromptu choruses that rang out whenever we passed a particularly malodorous pasture. My dad would begin with his deep bass, "Honey farm!" Mom would join the next round with her rich alto; the third go-around would be the kids' chorus; finally, Mark would pipe up with the last layer in his sweetly strident baby voice, "Hon - nee faaaaaaarrrrrrrrrrrrrmmm!" No matter how many times we repeated this totally inane ritual, we always laughed.

These remembrances of laughter and joy help to see us through the perilous times in the journey of life. It has become more and more evident to me as I observe the lives of other families that we are all fundamentally dysfunctional to some degree. As I read and reread the Bible year after year, the truth of this hits home: it all started with Adam and Eve. Their disobedience to God in the garden of Eden created the sinful nature that has been passed to and through every generation thereafter.

Early this morning, I was thinking about the veritable soap opera that is the story of Abraham and his family in the book of Genesis. Right after we are introduced to "Abram" in Genesis 11:27, whom God would later rename "Abraham," meaning "a father of many nations," we read chapter after chapter of a laundry list of sins and character flaws: Abram asks his wife Sarai to tell Pharaoh that she is his sister and not his wife so that Pharaoh will treat him well (a "white lie" because she was actually his half-sister); Sarai orders her maidservant Hagar to sleep with Abram so that she will not be shamed by her own infertility; Hagar bears Abram's son Ishmael through this unwed pregnancy; Sarai, by this time renamed Sarah, becomes miraculously pregnant at the age of ninety and bears a son, Isaac; the whole cycle of lies is repeated when they move to Gerar and Abraham claims to King Abimelech that Sarah is his sister, not his wife; Sarah becomes rabidly jealous of Hagar and Ishmael and orders Abraham to banish them.

The really interesting thing is that the entire cycle of deception, lies, and jealousy repeats itself in the next generation! Isaac marries Rebekah; they have twin sons, Esau and Jacob; Isaac deceives King Abimelech by telling him, just as his father Abraham did, that his wife is his sister; Rebekah urges the younger twin, Jacob, to deceive his father in order to get the blessing traditionally bestowed on the elder son, his brother Esau; Isaac manipulates Jacob to prevent him from marrying a Canaanite woman, just as Abraham had done to Isaac; Esau, out of rebellion towards his father in losing his birthright, goes to the banished Uncle Ishmael and marries his daughter; Jacob's new father-in-law, Laban, deceives him on his wedding night and substitutes his older daughter Leah for the more beautiful Rachel, the one whom Jacob had intended to marry.

Is your family looking pretty good at this point? I think mine is smelling like a rose! The amazing aspect to all of this is that God had chosen Abraham to be the father of many nations, and He blessed his seed despite the sins of the father which were passed down through the generations. There were dire consequences for these sins, but God extended His mercy and forgiveness because Abraham, Isaac, and Jacob kept coming back to Him. Jacob wrestled with God one night, saying, "I will not let you go unless you bless me" (Genesis 32:26). After receiving the blessing, he named the place Peniel, saying, "It is because I saw God face to face, and yet my life was spared" (Genesis 32:30).

One of the most touching stories follows in chapter 33, as Jacob looks up and sees Esau approaching with four hundred men. Terrified by the prospect of this confrontation with the brother he had so deceived, Jacob bows to the ground seven times in an act of contrite deference. But Esau runs to greet his brother and embraces him, even kissing him. He asks why all of Jacob's family members have come to greet him, and Jacob says, "To find favor in your eyes, my lord" (Genesis 33:8). Esau replies that he already has plenty, and urges his brother to keep what he has for himself. Jacob says, "No, please! If I have found favor in your eyes, accept this gift from me. For to see your face is like seeing the face of God, now that you have received me favorably. Please accept the present that was brought to you, for God has been gracious to me and I have all I need."(Genesis 33:10-11)

Family is about forgiveness. We are God's family, and "as a father has compassion on his children, so the Lord has compassion on those who fear Him. For He knows how we are formed; He remembers that we are dust. As for man, his days are like grass, he flourishes like a flower of the field; the wind blows over it and it is gone, and its place remembers it no more. But from everlasting to everlasting the Lord's love is with those who fear Him, and His righteousness with their children's children—with those who keep His covenant and remember to obey His precepts" (Psalm 103:13-18).

God knew that we were powerless to overcome our sinful nature, so He sent His Son as the New Covenant to break the law of sin and death.

> Therefore, there is now no condemnation for those who are in Christ Jesus, because through Christ Jesus the law of the Spirit of life set me free from the law of sin and death. For what the law was powerless to do in that it was weakened by the sinful nature, God did by sending His own Son in the likeness of sinful man to be a sin offering. And so He condemned sin in sinful man, in order that the righteous requirements of the law might be fully met in us, who do not live according to the sinful nature but according to the Spirit (Romans 8:1-4).

As Christians, we are grafted into a new family, the body of Christ, which is His church. We have a new identity in Christ, and are co-heirs with Him in the Kingdom of God. We are blessed with ready-made relationships because we share the blood of Jesus! Carrie and I took a divine short cut from strangers to sisters, even calling ourselves "twins," because we were both born again in Christ. And as part of the family of God, we all have the assurance of salvation and the knowledge that because of His presence in us, we are able to do exceedingly abundantly more than we can ask or even imagine according to His power that is at work within us (Ephesians 3:20).

I'm thanking God even as I finish this chapter for loving me as His daughter and placing me in His family. My heart is remembering Hans Naegeli's old hymn "Blest Be the Tie that Binds" that speaks of fellowship in the body of Christ, our family now and forever!

> Blest be the tie that binds
> our hearts in Christian love!
> The fellowship of kindred minds
> is like to that above.
> Before our Father's throne
> we pour our ardent prayers;
> Our fears, our hopes, our aims are one,
> Our comforts and our cares.
> We share our mutual woes,
> our mutual burdens bear;
> And often for each other flows
> the sympathizing tear.
> When we asunder part
> it gives us inward pain;
> But we shall still be joined in heart,
> and hope to meet again.

Loving Heavenly Father, what a privilege it is to know you as Abba, our Daddy—the compassionate, merciful and gracious Father who gave your only Son so that we might live as a family for eternity. Help us to love one another as you have first loved us, that we might see your Kingdom come on earth as it is in heaven. In Jesus' name, Amen.

Have I not commanded you? Be strong and courageous. Do not be terrified; do not be discouraged, for the Lord your God will be with you wherever you go. —Joshua 1:9

30

More than Conquerors

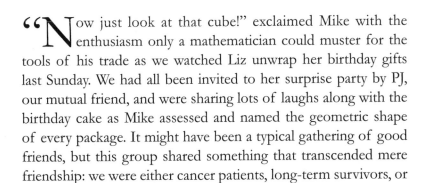

"Now just look at that cube!" exclaimed Mike with the enthusiasm only a mathematician could muster for the tools of his trade as we watched Liz unwrap her birthday gifts last Sunday. We had all been invited to her surprise party by PJ, our mutual friend, and were sharing lots of laughs along with the birthday cake as Mike assessed and named the geometric shape of every package. It might have been a typical gathering of good friends, but this group shared something that transcended mere friendship: we were either cancer patients, long-term survivors, or their spouses and caregivers.

Philippe and I had met PJ, our hostess, about five years ago when she came to the healing service at our church along with Liz, her close friend and caregiver. A long-term brain cancer patient, PJ continues to endure chemo and untold other procedures without complaint. She and Liz had been invited to the service by our friend and fellow church member Lynda, who has battled breast cancer with metastasis for several years. As we prayed together over the months and then years, the Lord bonded us in His love and has strengthened our faith as well as our bodies. Liz, herself a breast cancer survivor, came to know Jesus through these healing services.

I met Mike one Sunday afternoon last summer when I was asked by Pastor Stew Grant to lead the cancer support group in his absence. Mike had been diagnosed with glioblastoma, a virulent form of brain cancer, but the joy of the Lord was quite clearly his strength—and continues to be. A mathematics teacher at one of the local high schools, Mike has committed himself to sharing the love of Jesus with his students and colleagues. Although he was critically ill in December, his health has improved dramatically as he gives each day to the Lord's service. The peace of Christ dwells in him richly, not despite the circumstances, but because of them. He knows that "to live is Christ," and through Him, Mike is more than a conqueror.

Both Lynda and PJ can claim that title as well. Lynda is filled with grace and a gentle spirit, and an incandescent smile that warms my heart every time I see her. PJ might be considered the epitome of "spunk," with her steely determination, quick wit, and yet tender spirit, all wrapped up in about eighty pounds. When these two learned of our forthcoming trip to Uganda last spring, they were both determined to be missionaries right along with us as they undergirded Philippe, Paul and me with prayer. Lynda presented us with a check before we left to be used for the Lord's work there. We were able to purchase ninety dozen manuscript books—all that we could find—in the little village of Budaka for the children at the Compassion project, and they cheered when we delivered them. In turn, the children offered fervent prayers for PJ and Lynda, as well as for Carrie.

Our time in Uganda led to the establishment of the Uganda Book Project, which provides Christian and classic books to these precious people who have been inconceivably afflicted by the aftermath of the terrorist regime of Idi Amin in the 1970's, leaving many without family, homes, or the other basic necessities of life. In his book *A Distant Grief,* which describes the atrocities of this time in Uganda's history, F. Kefa Sempangi, a native Ugandan who became a believer and then a pastor during the Amin regime, tells of preaching a victorious Easter sermon in 1973 to seven thousand God-hungry worshipers gathered in an outdoor compound. After a final loud "Amen!" and chorus from the church choir, Sempangi made his way through the crowd to change his clothes in the vestry. Exhausted but exhilarated by what the Lord had done, he was preoccupied and did not notice five men behind him until they closed the door and pointed their rifles at his face. Sempangi immediately recognized them as Amin's Nubian assassins. "We are going to kill you. If you have something to say, say it before you die."[38]

Sempangi writes:

> I could only stare at him. For a sickening moment I felt the full weight of his rage. We had never met before but his deepest desire was to tear me to pieces. My mouth felt heavy and my limbs began to shake. Everything left my control. They will not need to kill me, I thought to myself. I am just going to fall over. I am going to fall over dead and I will never see my family again. I thought of Penina home alone with Damali. What would happen to them when I was gone?

> From far away I heard a voice, and I was astonished to realize that it was my own. "I do not need to plead my own cause," I heard myself saying. "I am a dead man already. My life is dead and hidden in Christ. It is your lives that are in danger, you are dead in your sins. I will pray to God that after you have killed me, He will spare you from eternal destruction."

> The tall one took a step towards me and then stopped. In an instant, his face was changed. His hatred had turned to curiosity. He lowered his gun and motioned to the others to do the same. They stared at him in amazement but they took their guns from my face. Then the tall one spoke again. "Will you pray for us

now?" he asked. I thought my ears were playing a trick. I looked at him and then at the others. My mind was completely paralyzed. The tall one repeated his question more loudly, and I could see that he was becoming impatient. "Yes, I will pray for you," I answered. My voice sounded bolder even to myself. "I will pray to the Father in heaven. Please bow your heads and close your eyes." The tall one motioned to the others again, and together the five of them lowered their heads. I bowed my own head, but I kept my eyes open. The Nubian's request seemed to me a strange trick. Any minute, I thought to myself, my life will end. I did not want to die with my eyes closed.

"Father in heaven," I prayed, "you who have forgiven men in the past, forgive these men also. Do not let them perish in their sins but bring them into yourself." It was a simple prayer, prayed in deep fear. But God looked beyond my fears and when I lifted my head, the men standing in front of me were not the same men who had followed me into the vestry. Something had changed in their faces. It was the tall one who spoke first. His voice was bold but there was no contempt in his words. "You have helped us," he said, "and we will help you. We will speak to the rest of our company and they will leave you alone. Do not fear for your life. It is in our hands and you will be protected."

I was too astonished to reply. The tall one only motioned for the others to leave. He himself stepped to the doorway and then he turned to speak one last time. "I saw widows and orphans in your congregation," he said. "I saw them singing and giving praise. Why are they happy when death is so near?" It was still difficult to speak but I answered him. "Because they are loved by God. He has given them life, and will give life to those they loved, because they died in Him."

I drove home that Easter evening deeply puzzled but with a joy in my heart. I felt that I had passed from death to life, and that I could now speak in one mind with Paul: "I have been crucified with Christ and I no longer live, but Christ lives in me. The life I live in the body, I live by faith in the Son of God, who loved me and gave Himself for me" (Galatians 2:20).[39]

Kefa Sempangi is, without a doubt, more than a conqueror. And whether the enemy comes under the guise of Nubian assassins or metastatic cancer, every believer in Christ has this identity.

My husband Philippe made a DVD of our trip to Uganda, a copy of which we gave to PJ on our return. She wrote an e-mail to me in response:

> Wow...I just finished watching the DVD. What a wonderful blessing you bestowed on me. It is hard right now to get my thoughts in some kind of order. But I do know for certain that God is very much alive in Africa. What a fine example of what a believer should be like. The Bible says we are to delight ourselves in the Lord, and have joy in the Lord. These people are a living testimony of just how much delight and joy there really is in serving the Lord. I was touched by the way they express their freedom in the Lord, each in their own special way. You can tell that they feel the presence of the Lord by the way they lift their eyes to heaven and touch their hearts while they sing. The smiles on their faces are just beautiful and radiate the love of Jesus. I caught myself tapping my hands and feet and humming along with them. You can't help but share in the enthusiasm of their worship.

Lynda and her daughter Whitley have been instrumental in collecting, sorting and cataloging books for the Uganda Book Project. Whitley asked that her friends bring books rather than gifts to her eleventh birthday party so that they could donate them to the Project. She even played our DVD at her party. Whitley and her mom joined our neighbor Sheri and her daughter Claire's Girl Scout troop in making and decorating library card inserts for the books. The very first shipment we sent to the Budaka Compassion Child Development Center was dedicated to the memory of Carrie Oliver.

How amazing it is to see God's promises in Romans 8 fulfilled! Although PJ, Lynda and Carrie were all cancer patients and traveling to Uganda was not an option for them, they fully participated in our journey by allowing the presence of Christ in them to make them more than conquerors—to not allow the circumstance of cancer to deter them from serving the Lord and from loving His children through their prayers.

CARRIE

Journal entry, September 27, 2005: "I command you—be strong and courageous! Do not be afraid or discouraged. For the Lord your God is with you wherever you go" (Joshua 1:9 NLT).

I began this update with a scripture on "courage." In church, once again the message had to be just for me! Pastor Mark talked about our understanding and experience with God as Sovereign, our trust in God, and our courage. These three areas affect us personally, in our circle of influence, and globally. I sat there on Saturday night and felt no trouble with my sovereign God or that I could trust Him, but the courage thing is hard! Courage is defined as "mental or moral strength to venture, persevere, and withstand danger, fear and difficulty." Then I thought again, "In order to be courageous, I have to believe that my sovereign God is with me. I have to trust that, and out of that experience He gives us courage."

It took courage to come home from Laguna Beach and the beautiful, safe and cozy little cottage. I wanted to stay there under my down comforter and breathe the salty air and forget about cancer for a very long time. It took courage to go back to chemo last week. I thank God for the gift of those that join me in that venture. It took courage to get up every day after chemo, knowing that not feeling well was probably pretty likely. Some days I had more courage than others, and on the very days that I lacked courage, those came to me and gave a gift—the gift of themselves. I thank God for this gift and for His promise that He will continue to go with me on this journey, never leaving my side, giving me the courage I need and the gifts of the Body of Christ.

Carrie was more than a conqueror. So is her husband Gary. As he has pressed on through more turbulent waters than many Christians will ever experience, he continues to profess his faith in God and to manifest His sovereign joy. As a cancer survivor himself, and the primary caregiver for Carrie, he has been subjected to the fiery furnace countless times, but has emerged as gold. I remember him asking with his wry sense of humor, "Isn't twenty-four carat enough, Lord?" Gary never complained about the relentless onslaught; he kept his eyes fixed on his Savior. Because of that, he has been able to be more than a conqueror.

He sent me an e-mail recently in which he mentioned the struggles that caregivers face when their loved ones are terminally ill:

> On a number of occasions, Carrie would take my hand in her frail hand, look at me with her still-beautiful green eyes, and tell me that there were few who understood or even thought about what the stress and strain and pressure (spiritual, physical, psychological, emotional, financial, etc.) must be like for me and that probably only she knew even a bit of the price I was paying. I hadn't really thought about it, but I remember the first time she said something like that to me, I started weeping. I felt a bit guilty even thinking about myself, but as a psychologist I knew enough to know that if I wanted to be strong for her for the long run, I'd better not be in denial or ignore the sustained stress and strain and spiritual warfare I was facing. In some ways the caregiver's price is nothing compared to the one with the disease, but there still is a price that the caregiver pays long after their loved one is gone, and

most caregivers receive no understanding or support for their needs.

Gary, even after such catastrophic loss, is focused on helping others who are walking through the valley of the shadow of death with their dear ones. He knows that as believers in Christ, we are all able to be more than conquerors through Him who has conquered the grave and won the victory over sin and death.

> **Sovereign Lord**, You have assured us that nothing can separate us from your love that is in Christ Jesus: neither death nor life, angels or demons, the present or the future, nor any powers, neither height nor depth nor anything else in all creation. With this assurance, Lord, we need not fear, for through the death and resurrection of Christ, we are redeemed and can live as more than conquerors! We pray this in Jesus' name, Amen.

[Note: Since the original writing of this manuscript, our dear friends Lynda Frank and Mike Sheridan have both gone on to find their complete healing in heaven. We cherish the memories and fruit of their beautiful lives.]

The Lord bless you and keep you; the Lord make His face shine upon you and be gracious to you; the Lord turn His face toward you and give you peace. —Numbers 6:24-26

31

Blessing

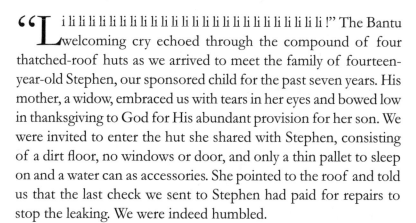

"Li li li li li li li li li li li li li li li li li li li li li li li li li li li !" The Bantu welcoming cry echoed through the compound of four thatched-roof huts as we arrived to meet the family of fourteen-year-old Stephen, our sponsored child for the past seven years. His mother, a widow, embraced us with tears in her eyes and bowed low in thanksgiving to God for His abundant provision for her son. We were invited to enter the hut she shared with Stephen, consisting of a dirt floor, no windows or door, and only a thin pallet to sleep on and a water can as accessories. She pointed to the roof and told us that the last check we sent to Stephen had paid for repairs to stop the leaking. We were indeed humbled.

Outside again, the extended family gathered as our family of three shared in fellowship with the tribal members and the Compassion International staff from the Budaka (Uganda) Child Development Center. Philippe pronounced a blessing on Stephen from Deuteronomy 28, and his mother in turn released Stephen to whatever care we were led to provide for him. She then presented us with her own gifts to our family: a live chicken and a bag of fresh fruit picked from their field. I was reminded of the offering of the widow in Mark 12:46, where Jesus said to the disciples, "They all gave out of their wealth, but she, out of her poverty, put in everything—all she had to live on."

The preceding paragraphs were excerpted from an article I wrote for Compassion International following our visit to Uganda in early June of 2007. One of the most profound moments of our time with Stephen's tribe in that little compound deep in the heart of Africa was when Philippe felt the prompting of the Holy Spirit to speak a blessing over our sponsored son and his family. He spoke extemporaneously but with the anointed authority that comes only from God:

> You will be blessed in the city and blessed in the country. You will be blessed when you come in and blessed when you go out. The Lord will send a blessing on your barns and on everything your put your hand to. The Lord will open the heavens, the storehouse of His bounty, to send rain on your land in season and to bless all the work of your hands (Deuteronomy 28:3, 6, 8, 12).

I could sense the impact of God's words as they fell on these people like a gentle spring rain on parched earth. They had been blessed.

I am very drawn to the passages of blessing and benediction in the Bible. Many are used as benedictions in church services, such as Numbers 6:24-26; in fact, the church that I attended as a young adult ended every service with the choir singing, "The Lord bless you and keep you…" I always left feeling the reassurance of that blessing. Another favorite is in Paul's prayer for the Ephesians, verses 20 and 21: "Now to Him who is able to do exceedingly abundantly more than all we can ask or even imagine, according to His power that is at work within us, to Him be glory in the church and in Christ Jesus throughout all generations, forever and ever! Amen." Now who would not be exhorted by that?! I love those double adverbs: "exceedingly abundantly"! That is the nature of the God we serve!

The brief book of Jude, just one chapter in length, ends with a call to persevere in faith in the midst of ungodliness:

> But you, dear friends, build yourselves up in your most holy faith and pray in the Holy Spirit. Keep yourselves in God's love as you wait for the mercy of our Lord Jesus Christ to bring you to eternal life. Be merciful to those who doubt; snatch others from the fire and save them; to others show mercy, mixed with fear— hating even the clothing stained by corrupted flesh (v. 20-23).

The very last sentence, however, is subtitled "Doxology"—praise to God. It is one of the most powerful benedictions I know:

> To Him who is able to keep you from falling and to present you before His glorious presence without fault and with great joy—to the only God our Savior be glory, majesty, power and authority, through Jesus Christ our Lord, before all ages, now and forevermore! Amen (v. 24-25).

That makes me want to shout to the hilltops! To clap my hands and dance! To fall on my face before my King! The thought of being presented "before His glorious presence without fault and with great joy" makes every trial in my life pale in comparison. I am living for that moment!

The idea of being blessed by God is one that isn't foreign to us, as it is entirely scriptural and is so much a part of being a child of our loving God. Blessing others, however, is not so common— unless you consider the perfunctory "Bless you!" one says after a sneeze. It is something that I have come to see as very significant in my own life, both as I am mentored by others in the faith and as I disciple those entrusted to me.

Before my dad died of prostate cancer in February of 2002,

he asked that each of his four children come to see him individually in the hospital. He felt very strongly that he was to bless each of us with words of affirmation and encouragement, and I will always remember the profound joy of knowing that my father was delighted with me! He also gave his blessing to my dear husband, as Philippe was truly a son to him, the apple of his eye. The power of his words helped to sustain us through our grief, and they inspire us even now.

One of the precious ones that God entrusted me to mentor was my young friend Zack Homrighaus, who had been diagnosed with glioblastoma as the age of seventeen. I sensed God urging me to write weekly letters to Zack with Bible passages for each of the days he would have radiation treatment. These letters were a blessing to Zack because he would take them along to the hospital and meditate on God's word as he was treated.

This young man grew into a mighty pillar of strength in the Lord over the four years that he lived after diagnosis. Countless lives were impacted by Zack's courage and testimony, and many of these people gathered at our church just two months before Zack died to pay tribute to him as his parents hosted a "Roast." We laughed, shared a scrumptious potluck meal, visited with others who had been indelibly impacted by his life, and then listened with rapt attention as his dad Ken pronounced a blessing on Zack. He told of the myriad emotions that had flooded the lives of his family over the past four years, and of how indescribably proud he was of his son. But the real clincher, and the moment when there were no dry eyes in the house, was when Ken said, "I think I feel like God must have felt after Jesus was baptized when He said, 'This is my Son, with Whom I am well-pleased.'" What a gift this blessing was to Zack!

Sometimes we are reluctant to fully invest ourselves in others if we know that we will only be part of their lives for a short season. One of my Rice University students, Rebecca, is serving as a missionary this summer to children in an orphanage in the

Philippines. She wrote in a recent e-mail:

> We've hit our halfway point in the trip, which I think presents a whole new set of challenges. I adore being here and getting to know and love these kids, but the reality that we only have three weeks left is setting in quickly. One of my teammates made an interesting observation the other day: we know we're only here a short time and the children know that we're only here for a short time, so is that fact keeping us from completely devoting ourselves to them because we don't want to get too attached? Are we not giving every bit of ourselves to them? And are they doing the same, only getting so close to us because they know we will leave and never come back? I've thought a lot about that the past few days, and honestly, I don't know if I'm holding myself back. My biggest prayer request this week is this: that we will be actively devoted to our work and these children as if our time here had no end....

As soon as I read this, I wrote back to Rebecca that her work is not temporal, but eternal. As she labors in the name of Jesus, these children are being loved with His love—the love that will last forever! She need not fear becoming too attached, because she is forming bonds with these precious little ones that will last for eternity.

Although I didn't meet Carrie until she had already been diagnosed with cancer, I never felt a sense of reserve about investing in our friendship. I felt that this was a divinely-appointed relationship that would bring untold blessings, both to me and to the body of Christ. Every moment we spent together, even if it was side by side in a sterile and impersonal treatment room, was cherished by both of us, because the Lord was always at the center. We trusted that God was able to heal her at any time, and we fervently prayed for that healing, but we also knew that

He was achieving in both Carrie and me an eternal glory that far outweighed the trials.

One of the "benefits" of having endured cancer is that every moment becomes more precious, not knowing how many might remain. The truth is that none of us knows how long we will live, whether we're presently healthy or not. God determines our days, and has written them in the Lamb's Book of Life. Our job is to live them to the fullest for His glory.

Carrie understood that, and she knew the importance of blessing, too. She was always affirming those she loved. Two days before she died, we had a phone conversation in which she gave me words of blessing for the unique friendship we had shared. Just two hours before she died, she asked her precious, longtime friend Cheryl Carmichael, who was at her bedside, to call me. I felt so blessed.

Carrie addressed some of her family members in a journal entry she wrote just before going to the Envita Center in Phoenix for treatment. She entitled this section, "Saying Goodbye," but it's really all about blessing.

CARRIE

Journal entry, March 4, 2006:

Goodbye Dear Mate. We have had tears and will have tears, but we will laugh as well and we will celebrate God's goodness and we will hug hard when we see each other in between, no matter if it is once or several times.

Goodbye Andrew. You don't have to be strong. Isn't that great to know? Remember to fly when you need to and God will meet you there.

Goodbye Matt and Amanda. I love you both. You are precious and you love me well with your notes and cards and gifts and words. Remember there is no fear in love.

Goodbye Miss Marsha. You are my sister and so precious to me. In your own pain and difficult circumstances, you still manage to love well. You definitely have wings to fly above your hardships.

So now we say goodbye, dear Carrie—for a time. You have fought the good fight, finished the course, and kept the faith. You have been blessed and you have been a blessing beyond description. You have lived and loved well. You have been presented before His glorious presence without fault and with great joy. We will see you in Glory.

Most gracious God, bless the Lord, O my soul; let all that is within me bless your holy name! Thank you for blessing your children with life that will never perish through the gift of your Son, our Savior and Lord Jesus Christ, now and forevermore. Amen.

As the Father has loved me, so have I loved you. Now remain in my love. If you obey my commands, you will remain in my love; just as I have obeyed my Father's commands and remain in His love. I have told you this so that my joy may be in you and that your joy may be complete. My command is this: Love each other as I have loved you. —John 15:9-11

32

Joy

C ARRIE
Journal entry, December 4, 2006: In this journey of cancer and walking through the valley of the shadow, God has been kind and gracious with me in the pain and sorrow, the difficulty of chemo, radiation, weight loss, sadness, and more reality than I care to experience. Just when I am tempted to think it is too much, He gives me good gifts that bring my heart joy. You see, I have passed from the life I knew before cancer to this present life that has been full of surprises that only God could allow and give to bring joy in the midst of sorrow. In this new place, God continues to delight my heart with the love of old friends and the love of new friends. He gives me power when I am so weak. He has given me a sense of my surroundings that fills my soul with a love for life that makes me weep, and He gives me a gala night with my prince.

I don't believe that I ever realized the pinnacle of true joy until I had traversed the valley of sorrow. I understood happiness: the cozy comfort of being well-fed, nicely clothed, and living in a more than decent dwelling. I appreciated pleasure: a delectable meal, a beautiful view, a concert of great music. I comprehended love: God's protection and provision, a caring family, supportive friends. But authentic joy was to be found somewhere I had never anticipated: I would discover it on the Via Dolorosa—the road of suffering. It would be the joy of Jesus.

What does that joy look like? Gary Oliver describes it so succinctly in his "Sovereign Joy" message:

> Circumstances don't determine reality...Joy is completely independent of all the chances and changes of life. Joy does not anesthetize us from reality, but reminds us of a greater Reality. Joy does not show up in spite of, but in the midst of tough times. Joy is an awareness of God's power, promises, and presence.[40]

Oswald Chambers writes in *My Utmost for His Highest* in the August 31st entry:

> The joy of Jesus was the absolute self-surrender and self-sacrifice of Himself to His Father; the joy of doing that which the Father sent Him to do. "I delight to do Thy will." Jesus prayed that our joy might go on fulfilling itself until it was the same joy as His. Have I allowed Jesus Christ to introduce his joy to me? The full flood of my life is not in bodily health, not in external happenings, not in seeing God's work succeed, but in the perfect understanding of God, and in the communion with Him that Jesus Himself had...Be rightly related to God, find your joy there, and out of you will flow rivers of living water.[41]

That scripture reference to "rivers of living water," John 7:38, is one that the Holy Spirit impressed on me to share with Carrie on March 14, 2007. As I prayed for her on my walk that morning, I was led to the passage in Exodus 15 in which Moses was leading the Israelites through the Desert of Shur. For three days they were unable to find water, and when they finally came to Marah, they could not drink the water because it was bitter. When Moses cried out to the Lord, he was shown a piece of wood which he threw into the water, and it became sweet. Then the Lord tested them by saying, "If you listen carefully to the voice of the Lord your God and do what is right in His eyes, if you pay attention to His commands and keep all His decrees, I will not bring on you any of the diseases I brought on the Egyptians, for I am the Lord who heals you" (Exodus15:26). Immediately after this, Moses and the Israelites came to Elim, where they found twelve springs of water and seventy palm trees, and they camped there beside the water.

I told Carrie that I sensed that the accumulating fluid in her abdomen was like the stagnant water of Marah, and that the Lord would replace it with His rivers of living water, which would flow from her to refresh others. A month later, she phoned on a Sunday morning in great distress, and Philippe and I prayed with her, asking the Lord to bring "streams of living water" from her belly. She had also prayed with two other intercessors.

CARRIE

Journal entry, April 17, 2007: I went to bed Sunday evening and slept so soundly, so deeply that I cannot remember much about the night. When I awoke in the morning, my stomach was half the size it was the day before, and it still is much smaller. Oh, how I have been given a glimpse of walking with my Lord on this earth. A glimpse of experiencing His perfect love, of feeling no fear, of the miracle of His presence.

So, is it a glimpse? Or is it possibly how He ultimately wants and desires for us to live? I think it is not a glimpse. It is the heaven on earth He wants for us. Oh, the power of this; oh, the love of this; oh, the transformation of this experience. Have you thought about how you have lived heaven today? If you did, how did you do that? If you don't think you did, what might be different about your life if you did live heaven on this earth? I know that God's power, God's healing hand, His presence, His leading, His playfulness and joy, His wisdom and discernment, His intimacy and more, are all the experiences of what it feels like, looks like, to live heaven on earth.

Carrie had learned that joy is the other side of the tapestry of life. Those broken threads of sorrow that appear to be random and disconnected are brought together on the opposite side in God's magnificent creative work of art. In Bob Sorge's *Secrets of the Secret Place*, he writes of Paul's prayer that "the Colossian believers would be 'strengthened with all might, according to His glorious power, for all patience and longsuffering with joy'" (Colossians 1:11). Sorge continues:

> One of the greatest challenges, in the place of hardship, is to suffer a long time WITH JOY. It's not possible in human strength! Which is why Paul prayed that they might be "strengthened with all might," for it takes the might of God to rejoice through long durations of painful hardship. Being joyful in suffering is a godly quality, for God Himself is "patience and longsuffering with joy." Consider how much God suffers as he shares the grief of the world and for how long He has thus suffered! And yet, although His suffering is stronger than any of us realize, He is also filled with great joy. Only God can suffer so much with such joy.[42]

It is really a complete contradiction of what the world would have us believe. "Suffer to find joy? Well, count me out!" The truth is that those who do not yet know Christ do not have the power of the Holy Spirit at work within them to guide, encourage and comfort. The disciples were taught this by Jesus when they shared their final meal together before He was betrayed:

> But the Counselor, the Holy Spirit, whom the Father will send in my name, will teach you all things and will remind you of everything I have said to you. Peace I leave with you; my peace I give you. I do not give to you as the world gives. Do not let your hearts be troubled, and do not be afraid (John 14:26-27).

> I have told you this so that my joy may be in you and that your joy may be complete. My command is this:

Love each other as I have loved you. Greater love has no one than this, that one lay down his life for his friends. You are my friends if you do what I command. I no longer call you servants, because a servant does not know his master's business. Instead I have called you friends, for everything that I learned from my Father I have made known to you. You did not choose me, but I chose you to go and bear fruit—fruit that will last. Then the Father will give you whatever you ask in my name. This is my command: Love each other (John 15:11-17).

To have joy is to know Jesus, to love Him, and to love one another as He first loved us. It is to abide in Him as a branch abides in the vine. It is to bear fruit that will have Kingdom-changing impact. It is to shine with the radiance of the Son. In Gary Oliver's journal update of May 1, 2008, he shares words of encouragement sent to him by a friend:

I bless you, and pray that your broken hearts be healed hearts. As you live in the depths of the deepest wells, may you find His light in the darkness—His joy in your sorrow, His glory in your valley. As you sow 'liquid prayers' in your tears, as you 'plant' seeds through the ministry of tears of sorrow, of travail, of desperation, of compassion—may you reap a harvest of spiritual breakthroughs, experience a spirit of rejoicing and spiritual harvest of great joy.[43]

Hannah Hurnard wrote a wonderful poem entitled "Joy" in her book *Walking Among the Unseen*. It summarizes what I know to be absolutely true—joy is sorrow overcome by the blood of Jesus:

> Hark to Love's triumphant shout!
> Joy is born from pain;
> Joy is sorrow inside out;
> Grief remade again.

Broken hearts, look up and see;
This is Love's own victory.

Here marred things are made anew,
Filth is here made clean;
Here are robes, not rags for you,
Mirth where tears have been.
Where sin's dreadful power was found,
Grace doth now much more abound!

Hark! Such songs of jubilation,
Every creature sings!
Great the joy of every nation,
Love is King of kings.
See, ye blind ones! Shout ye dumb!
Joy is sorrow overcome.[44]

Heavenly Father, You have turned our mourning into
dancing, and given us a garment of praise for a spirit of
despair. We rejoice in who we are in you: the redeemed
sons and daughters of the Most High! Let your joy be
our strength as we love one another with the love you
have first shown us. In Jesus' name, Amen.

Praise be to the God and Father of our Lord Jesus Christ, the Father of compassion and the God of all comfort, who comforts us in all our troubles, so that we can comfort those in any trouble with the comfort we ourselves have received from God. For just as the sufferings of Christ flow over into our lives, so also through Christ our comfort overflows. — II Corinthians 1:3-5

33

Compassion

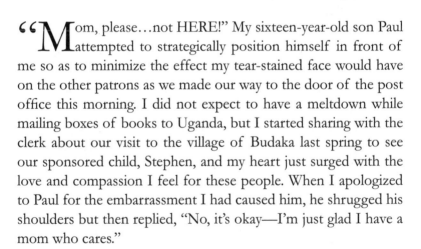

"Mom, please...not HERE!" My sixteen-year-old son Paul attempted to strategically position himself in front of me so as to minimize the effect my tear-stained face would have on the other patrons as we made our way to the door of the post office this morning. I did not expect to have a meltdown while mailing boxes of books to Uganda, but I started sharing with the clerk about our visit to the village of Budaka last spring to see our sponsored child, Stephen, and my heart just surged with the love and compassion I feel for these people. When I apologized to Paul for the embarrassment I had caused him, he shrugged his shoulders but then replied, "No, it's okay—I'm just glad I have a mom who cares."

I've heard it said that if you want something done, ask a busy person. Perhaps there is a corollary in matters of the heart: if you want someone who cares, ask a person who has known hardship. We are born as self-centered individuals with a sinful nature who at first think that the entire universe revolves around us. We are totally helpless and require enormous amounts of love and care. At some point, sooner or later, reality hits home and we start to become aware of those around us and their own needs. Some choose to extend themselves and help others, and some continue to indulge the desires of their flesh.

In an excerpt that I found in the *Devotional Classics* anthology, Jonathan Edwards, an eighteenth-century American theologian who was instrumental in the "Great Awakening" revival, spoke of "affections" that we have by nature:

> The nature of human beings is to be inactive unless influenced by some affection: love or hatred, desire, hope, fear, etc. These affections are the "spring of action," the things that set us moving in our lives, that move us to engage in activities. When we look at the world, we see that people are exceedingly busy. It is their affections that keep them busy. If we were to take away their affections, the world would be motionless and dead; there would be no such thing as activity. It is the affection we call covetousness that moves a person to seek worldly profits; it is the affection we call ambition that moves a person to pursue worldly glory; it is the affection we call lust that moves a person to pursue sensual delights. Just as worldly affections are the spring of worldly actions, so the religious affections are the spring of religious actions. A person who has a knowledge of doctrine and theology only—without religious affection—has never engaged in true religion. Nothing is more apparent than this: our religion takes root within us only as deep as our affections attract it. There are thousands who hear the Word of God, who hear great and exceedingly important truths about themselves and their lives, and yet all they hear has no effect upon them, makes no change in the way they live. The reason is this: they are not affected with what they hear. There are many who hear about the power, the holiness, and the wisdom of God; about Christ and the great things that He has done for them and

His gracious invitation to them; and yet they remain exactly as they are in life and in practice. I am bold in saying this, but I believe that no one is ever changed, either by doctrine or teaching of another, unless the affections are moved by these things. No one ever seeks salvation, no one ever cries for wisdom, no one ever wrestles with God, no one ever kneels in prayer or flees from sin, with a heart that remains unaffected. In a word, there is never any great achievement by the things of religion without a heart deeply affected by those things.[45]

Before I had cancer, I didn't really understand suffering very well. I remember thinking to myself at a much younger age, "If I ever had cancer, I think I would feel so…unclean; kind of polluted." Even as an adult, I was rather uncomfortable around those who had that diagnosis, and practiced quite a bit of assiduous hand-washing if I had to be around them. Then I got to walk in those shoes myself, and talk about a paradigm shift! I wondered how I would be treated if all of my hair fell out in clumps, my skin grew sickeningly sallow, or my body was consumed and emaciated. I wondered if my husband would still find me attractive and desirable. I wondered most of all if I could tolerate my own imperfections.

In the process of being treated for cancer, my "affections" underwent a radical transformation. I gradually became more and more aware that my life was really not my own, but a gift from God to be used to show His love to this needy world. God had not stricken me with this disease, but He promised through His word that He would work it all together for good because of my love for Him and the call He had for my life (Romans 8:28).

CARRIE

Journal entry, February 6, 2006: This dedication goes out to the many people that I have been praying for with cancer that have come into my life since my diagnosis: Sonia, Tonya, Nadine, Rosalee, Audrey, Shedd, Nancy Hardin,

Wade, Jane's mom, Sue Ann, Larry, Mark's uncle, Dick Rezzonico, Jake, the precious young blonde woman I saw at MDA, Jan, my Mom, my sister Chris, my brother-in-law Mike, and my husband Gary, who are all survivors. I know there have been more but these are the ones coming to mind right now. Remember, you are not alone! Be blessed, dear ones, as you fight, as you learn more about the great Healer who loves you deeply, who has vast mercy and grace for you each day and who wants you to experience His "sovereign joy" in the midst of the struggle.

Nearly two decades after my own diagnosis, I look back on the ways in which the Lord has opened up my heart with compassion towards others who suffer. The richness that has come into my life as a result of being allowed to "share in the sufferings of Christ" (I Peter 4:13) cannot be measured. It is mind-boggling for me to think that it was because of my own unsought experience with cancer that I was asked to help Carrie through her journey, and was blessed beyond description when our relationship became a sisterhood! The fourth chapter of I Peter begins, "Therefore, since Christ suffered in His body, arm yourselves also with the same attitude, because He who has suffered in his body is done with sin. As a result, he does not live the rest of his earthly life for evil human desires, but rather for the will of God" (v. 1-2). This is the "affection" of compassion.

Jonathan Edwards continued in his treatise on "Religious Affections" to expound on this:

> The Holy Scriptures also speak of compassion as an essential affection in true religion, so much so that all of the good characters in the Bible demonstrate it. The Scriptures choose this quality as the one which will determine who is righteous: "The righteous show mercy" (Psalm 37:21). It is our way of honoring God: "He that honors the Lord shows mercy to the poor" (Proverbs 14:31). Jesus Himself said it is the way we obtain mercy: "Blessed are the merciful, for they shall

receive mercy" (Matthew 5:7).[46]

Paul exhorts the saints at Philippi, and of course, all believers, to work out our salvation with fear and trembling (Philippians 2:12), having the same attitude as Christ:

> If you have any encouragement from being united with Christ, if any comfort from His love, if any fellowship with the Spirit, if any tenderness and compassion, then make my joy complete by being like-minded, having the same love, being one in spirit and purpose. Do nothing out of selfish ambition or vain conceit, but in humility consider others better than yourselves. Each of you should look not only to your own interests, but also to the interests of others (Philippians 2:1-5).

While we were in Uganda, the director of the Compassion center in Budaka, a native Ugandan and widowed mother of two sons, expressed her concern to us as we were sitting together outside talking with Stephen and the pastor, who was overseer of the Compassion project, about Stephen's future. When Stephen expressed a desire to be a doctor someday, Margaret looked at us with deeply questioning eyes and said, "But where will he get the books?" We hadn't realized that most of the teaching in that country is by rote due to the scarcity of books of any genre.

When we asked what might be done to help him, she pointed across the broad field to a compound of low-lying buildings. "That is a private school where he could receive the kind of education that might enable him to become a doctor." Philippe and I looked at each other and nodded in tacit agreement. The next thing we knew, the six of us—Stephen and Paul, Margaret and the pastor, Philippe and I—were all traipsing across the field towards the compound. We found the headmaster of the school and squeezed into his tiny office for an impromptu meeting. Within about thirty minutes, he had arranged for Stephen to be interviewed and tested the next morning at 7:30. By noon the next day, we were headed to the Budaka open-air village market to buy shoes, bedding, and school supplies for Stephen. Because his mother had given us her permission and blessing the day before to do anything we felt led by God to do for her son, we knew that this step would be approved by her, despite it necessitating her son boarding at the school. The joy from a smile that could light a thousand villages was all the reward we needed. Stephen was on his way. God had shown him compassion and had allowed us to come along for the ride!

C.S. Lewis once said that "the Son of God became a man so that men could become sons of God." The only way I could begin to comprehend the meaning of life was by understanding the depth of God's passion for me through the sacrifice of His sinless Son; then my own suffering takes on new meaning. The prophetic words of Isaiah foretold the profound persecution that Jesus would endure:

> He was despised and rejected by men; a man of sorrows, and familiar with suffering. Like one from whom men hide their faces He was despised, and we esteemed Him not. Surely He took up our infirmities and carried our sorrows, yet we considered Him stricken by God, smitten by Him, and afflicted. But He was pierced for our transgressions; He was crushed for our iniquities; the punishment that brought us peace was upon Him, and by His wounds we are healed. We all like sheep have gone astray; each of us has turned to his own way; and the Lord has laid on Him the iniquity of us all (Isaiah 53:3-6).

God has not in any way punished or persecuted me; it was the punishment that belonged to me which He willingly took from me so that His peace would be upon me! Out of gratitude for His mercy, it has become a privilege to offer my body as a living sacrifice to God. I feel so blessed when I have an opportunity to comfort another with the same comfort I have received from God as an outgrowth of being conformed to the image of Christ. One of the greatest joys of my life is to encourage other children of our heavenly Father to grow into the head that is Christ.

I made a hospital visit last Sunday to see a relatively young man who had suffered a massive stroke and then required brain surgery. As I stood with his anxious and frightened family in the ICU, the Lord urged me to ask if I could pray over him, and as I laid my hand on his paralyzed left arm, the presence of the Holy Spirit came over me. Tears began streaming down my face as I prayed words of life over him, and after a few minutes we were astonished to hear him whisper, "Hallelujah!" Believing with all my heart that God inhabits our praises and especially when we sing, I began to do just that. Even through my thick throat and salty tears, the Holy Spirit ministered to this dear man as I sang over and over, "Alleluia...alleluia...alleluia...alleluia...I will praise you, alleluia... you are worthy...alleluia." Imagine my joy when the next words he uttered were "Glory to the Lamb!" That was my cue to sing "Glory...glory...glory to the Lamb! Worthy...worthy...worthy is the Lamb! For the Lord is great, and worthy of all praise; the Lamb upon His throne! And unto you, we lift our voice in praise: the Lamb upon His throne!" This precious saint entered into the glory of the Lord the following night. How gracious of God to allow me to help usher him into the Kingdom!

This evening as I was walking our dogs and mulling over the events of the day, I was reflecting on the words of John Donne, the early 17th century poet, from his Meditation XVII:

> No man is an island, entire of itself; every man is a piece of the continent, a part of the main; if a clod be washed away by the sea, Europe is the less, as well as if a promontory were, as well as if a manor of thy friends or of thine own were; any man's death diminishes me, because I am involved in mankind; and therefore never send to know for whom the bell tolls; it tolls for thee.[47]

We do need one another. We are to rejoice with those who rejoice, and mourn with those who mourn, living in harmony with one another. We are not to be proud, but willing to associate with people of low position. We are not to repay evil for evil, but are to do what is right in the eyes of everyone. We are not to be overcome by evil, but are to overcome evil with good (Romans 12:15-18; 21). We are to become just like Jesus.

> **Glorious and gracious God**, there is none righteous, save you—but you have redeemed us by the blood of the Lamb and made us co-heirs with Christ. Help us to love one another with the love that you first showed us; to live lives of compassion that are worthy of the identity you have given us in Christ. We ask in Jesus' name, Amen.

Do not merely listen to the word, and so deceive yourselves. Do what it says. Anyone who listens to the word but does not do what it says is like a man who looks at his face in a mirror and, after looking at himself, goes away and immediately forgets what he looks like. But the man who looks intently into the perfect law that gives freedom, and continues to do this, not forgetting what he has heard, but doing it—he will be blessed in what he does.
—James 1:22

34

Obedience

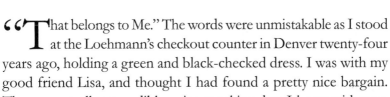

"That belongs to Me." The words were unmistakable as I stood at the Loehmann's checkout counter in Denver twenty-four years ago, holding a green and black-checked dress. I was with my good friend Lisa, and thought I had found a pretty nice bargain. There was really no audible voice speaking, but I knew without a doubt whose it was. I had just come through an intense time of realization that my brief first marriage was not within the will of God and had repented of my sin and rediscovered my faith. The Lord had rescued me, and now He was evidently speaking to me. But a dress? Where did that fit in? Surely God did not want my dress!

I completed my transaction and took my purchase home. There was no joy in me as I hung it in my already-overstuffed closet and mulled over those words I had heard. I prayed, "Lord, what are you trying to tell me?" The answer came quickly: "Tithe." I was to begin to tithe my monthly income, despite the uncertainty of my livelihood as a pianist after the accident that had permanently injured the tendons in my right arm. This was pretty terrifying to me, since I worked on a freelance basis with no guarantee of income each month, and had just purchased a new condominium on my own. The sense was so pervasive, though, that I knew I had to be obedient. What I didn't anticipate was that the Lord would do exactly what He promises to do in Malachi 3:10, "Bring the whole tithe into the storehouse, that there may be food in my house. Test me in this and see if I will not throw open the floodgates of heaven and pour out so much blessing that you will not have room enough for it."

As I conscientiously tallied up my receipts month after month and wrote checks to my church for ten percent, I also watched in amazement as the numbers increased! The Lord was blessing me for my obedience to His voice. Unbeknownst to me at the time, one of the deacons responsible for collecting and counting the tithes and offerings at church was...Philippe de Chambrier!

In a way that only God could orchestrate, I was asked by our pastor, Mark Brewer, to share my testimony of God's provision on Stewardship Sunday, and the only person I remember seeing in the congregation was Philippe! I had admired him for quite some time, but didn't know him very well, and wished he would ask me out. He came up to me afterwards and was very moved by my testimony. The rest is obvious: in time, he asked me to marry him. Talk about opening the floodgates of heaven! Not only that, but the Lord completely healed and restored my injured arm. That green and black-checked dress became a marker of God's faithfulness to His promises. Although I had disobeyed by purchasing it, I heard the Lord's voice, repented, and acted in obedience.

In her book *Walking Among the Unseen*, Hannah Hurnard addresses this matter of listening to God:

> In the Hebrew language hearing and obeying are the same word. Every Hebrew-speaking mother says to her child, "Hear me!" when she wants to say, "Now do what I tell you." That is why it is so important for us to remember that in the Bible sense of the word, faith includes obedient response. If we do not respond obediently to the Savior, we are not exercising true faith. To believe things about Him only has

to do with the intellect, but to respond in obedience is faith, exercised not simply in the mind, but in the very heart or will.

These days belief and faith are so often supposed to mean mere acceptance of the Christian doctrines and teaching, and acknowledging them as true and much better than the teaching and doctrines of any other religion. That of course is the beginning of faith; for who is going to step out and commit himself completely to One in whom he has no real confidence and whose teaching he does not really believe? But intellectual confidence is shown to be living faith which puts us in vital contact with all the power of God when we begin to respond in fullest obedience to our Lord and Savior. The Lord Himself said, "My sheep hear my voice," and if we know that we hear His voice and seek to obey it, this is the first positive proof that we have really been born again. Yet how many professing Christians admit sorrowfully that they have the greatest possible difficulty in getting guidance because they cannot distinguish if the ideas that come to them are God's voice or their own thoughts.[48]

I can speak to that from my own experience. The voice that I know to be that of God is never, ever condemning. Convicting, yes—but never condemning. It is Satan, the father of lies, who puts ideas in our heads of inadequacy, worthlessness, and failure. His modus operandi is to try to separate us from communicating with God by cultivating the impulses of the flesh. We get on a carousel of condemnation that whirls faster and faster until we feel helpless and hopeless.

CARRIE

Journal entry, January 6, 2007: We must be aware of fervently cultivating belief and hope that God loves us in the midst of joy, happiness, sorrow and pain. In the here and now of the day, we are to be very aware of the spiritual battle that wages. Satan is fighting for our thoughts, totally invested in defeating our minds as well as our hearts, and finally to separate us from the love and truth of who God is. That is why he exists: to separate us from God. If I get stuck in the "what if," I risk becoming separated from God.

I was not walking closely with the Lord when I married my first husband. The night before the wedding, God was moving heaven and earth to try to show me that this was not His will for my life. I even told my fiance that I did not love him, but he told me that I was just nervous and would get over it. I was so overcome by a sense of unworthiness that I told him maybe he was right—but deep down, I didn't feel that I deserved anyone better.

The day of the wedding dawned with torrential thunderstorms, almost as if my heavenly Father were sobbing over me. I recall standing alone before a full-length mirror at my parents' church, wearing my mother's exquisite wedding gown, thinking despondently, "This is the biggest mistake of my life." What I didn't fully realize was that God was providing a way out, even as He promises in I Corinthians 10:13, "No temptation has seized you except what is common to man. And God is faithful; He will not let you be tempted beyond what you can bear. But when you are tempted, He will also provide a way out so that you can stand up under it." God was keeping His promise by "speaking" to me through the wind and the rain, flooding the streets so that the ceremony had to be delayed by a half-hour, and through that sickening feeling in the pit of my stomach that I was not walking in obedience.

Since that time, I have attuned myself to God's voice through immersion in His word every day, being in right relationship with Him through confession and repentance of my sins, and praying and worshiping both individually and corporately. I have learned that He speaks often to me through the Bible, through other committed believers, through life circumstances, and through that still, small voice that is always gentle, loving, and yet firm and convicting.

I have had countless opportunities to test my ability to hear God's voice, and the stakes seem to get higher and higher as the years go by. I know that it is God's fervent desire for us to be conformed to the image of His Son, and in order to do that, we must model ourselves after Jesus. "I do nothing on my own but speak just what the Father has taught me" (John 8:28). In order to be taught, we must know that we hear Him correctly.

It was on Wednesday, February 19 of 2003 that I "heard" the Lord's voice speaking insistently to me during my morning prayer time. I had made an appointment with Dr. Richard Harper, a pre-eminent neurological surgeon in Houston, for a surgical consultation because I was in unrelenting, agonizing pain from two herniated disks in my neck after the roller-blading accident I had in October, 2000. Although I had phoned his office in early January, there was no available appointment until Friday, February 21, which happened to be my birthday.

On that Wednesday morning as I prayed, I sensed the entire direction of my plans changing; that the Lord was telling me to cancel the appointment with the surgeon. I said, "Lord, I know your voice, and I believe that this is what you're telling me to do. I don't usually ask you for a "fleece" (I was referring to the story of Gideon in Judges 6), but if this is truly what you're saying to me, then I'd like for YOU to have Dr. Harper's office call ME and cancel the appointment! And just to confirm it, if you would have them call sooner rather than later, I could make other plans for my birthday!"

Just forty-five minutes later, the phone rang and it was none other than Dr. Harper's secretary calling to say that he had a surgery unexpectedly scheduled for the time of my appointment on Friday. When she asked if I'd like to reschedule, I said "No thanks!" and hung up the phone shouting "Hallelujah!" Although I was still in every bit as much pain, I knew that God had a different plan to heal my neck. For two more months there was no change, but one day in April, I awakened with something conspicuously missing: pain! At first I thought perhaps it was just a respite for one day, but it soon became evident that the Lord had healed me of my affliction. He had spoken to me, I had listened, and I acted in obedience.

God used this experience to build my faith. "Faith comes from hearing the message, and the message is heard through the word of Christ" (Romans 10:17). My job is to walk in obedience, and the Lord does the rest. I have learned the truth of Isaiah's prophetic words in chapter 55:

> "For my thoughts are not your thoughts, neither are your ways my ways," declares the Lord. "As the heavens are higher than the earth, so are my ways higher than your ways and my thoughts than your thoughts. As the rain and the snow come down from heaven, and do not return to it without watering the earth and making it bud and flourish, so that it yields seed for the sower and bread for the eater, so is my word that goes out from my mouth: It will not return to me empty, but will accomplish what I desire and achieve the purpose for which I sent it" (Isaiah 55:8-11).

All we have to do is listen—and obey.

Gracious God, there is no better place to be than in the center of your will, hearing your voice and walking in obedience. Thank you for loving me so personally and intimately that I can know your voice and trust you to lead me in your ways. In Jesus' name, Amen.

And I heard a loud voice from the throne saying, "Now the dwelling of God is with men, and He will live with them. They will be His people, and God Himself will be with them and be their God. He will wipe every tear from their eyes. There will be no more death or mourning or crying or pain, for the old order of things has passed away." —Revelation 21:3

35

Anniversaries

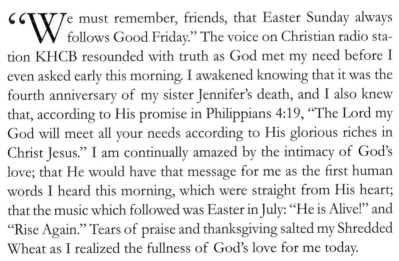

"We must remember, friends, that Easter Sunday always follows Good Friday." The voice on Christian radio station KHCB resounded with truth as God met my need before I even asked early this morning. I awakened knowing that it was the fourth anniversary of my sister Jennifer's death, and I also knew that, according to His promise in Philippians 4:19, "The Lord my God will meet all your needs according to His glorious riches in Christ Jesus." I am continually amazed by the intimacy of God's love; that He would have that message for me as the first human words I heard this morning, which were straight from His heart; that the music which followed was Easter in July: "He is Alive!" and "Rise Again." Tears of praise and thanksgiving salted my Shredded Wheat as I realized the fullness of God's love for me today.

Anniversaries are commemorations of the landmark moments in our lives: birthdays and weddings are joyous occasions that we look forward to celebrating with family and friends. They become all the more precious to us when we are thrust into the awareness of the impermanence of life on earth. Celebration takes on a poignant fervor.

CARRIE

Journal entry, January 6, 2006: That evening of (December) the 27th, Gary and I went out on a magical and romantic 25th wedding anniversary dinner. When we arrived we were greeted and escorted to our table to find a vase of cream roses (the flower of the Delta Gamma sorority) given to us by three of the DG's, and a bottle of champagne in a bucket, a gift from my sister Chris. The waiter was such a great sport, taking many pictures of us, and then we ate to our hearts' content. Thank you, Lord, for my husband of 25 years! I gave him a scuba diving trip and he gave me diamond earrings. I know I got the best deal! I will not forget Christmas, 2005.

We also commemorate those epic events that rock our lives with a seismic force that forever changes us: the death of a loved one; the diagnosis of cancer.

CARRIE

Journal entry, May 15, 2006: Looking around my room in Phoenix, I see reminders of a year and a journey that will probably mark my life here on this earth as the greatest adventure, battle, growth experience, witness of God's hand and love and mercy, heart-to-heart connection with the Body of Christ, emotions of all sorts, and more. In this anniversary week, we walked through finding out that the tumor was inoperable and that I had a positive lymph node in my neck. All of these experiences could add up to trauma, tragedy and crisis. Certainly in my experience of being a human I felt these things, but what I know to be true and what I celebrate with this one-year anniversary is that there was a moment where I came face to face with my Lord Jesus Christ and we talked about my choices—and really, there were only two. One choice would be to succumb to the trauma and tragedy of it all and sink into a deep, dark, angry, depressed state and perhaps give up and give in to the statistics of the cancer that was growing in my body. The other choice, and I remember it well, was to "choose" to cling tightly to Jesus and to "live" desperately needing Him 24 hours a day and trusting that He would be there for me, just as His scriptures have promised for thousands of years. Scriptures that I would

*have said I believed but didn't always function like I believed them. Psalm 91
became my Psalm to trust in and believe to be true. The Lord is my shelter;
He will protect me from the dangers of the day and the terrors of the night;
He keeps me on a straight path; I can stomp on the serpents that seek to at-
tack me; He places me in the hands of the angels to hold me; He promises me
a long life and salvation. This Psalm has sustained me over and over again
throughout this year.*

God's word and the faithfulness of His presence and promises
have sustained my family and me through our profound losses as
well. Sometimes God manifests His presence in a way we don't expect, and He gives us a profound reassurance that He is in control,
even in the midst of the valley of the shadow of death. Exactly two
weeks before my sister took her life, I was lying in bed one night
and suddenly saw an image of billowy, cumulous clouds, rather
like a child's impression of heaven. As I stared at those clouds
in wonder, an enormous surreal stoplight imposed itself on the
peaceful image. Unlike most stoplights, this had only a red and a
green light—no yellow. Both lights were illuminated. Startled by
this vision, I prayed Jeremiah 33:3, calling on the Lord to tell me
those "great and unsearchable things" I did not know. The Holy
Spirit gave me only a scripture verse at that moment, which was
Mark 3:25, "If a house is divided against itself, that house cannot
stand." I was thoroughly puzzled, but based on prior experience,
I knew to write it down and allow the Lord to reveal its meaning
in His time.

All was forgotten when we received the anguished call from
my mom on Sunday, July 18, 2004 that Jennifer had taken her life.
In the midst of agonizing pain unlike any I had ever experienced,
we moved in a surreal fast-forward mode to make plans to fly to
Chicago, take care of funeral arrangements, and clean out Jenn's
apartment. The immediate crisis took precedence over all else and
we operated on God's grace, providing moment by moment for
every need. Our precious friends Lisa and Andy Norman cut their

vacation with family short and drove down from Michigan to face the Herculean task of sorting through all of Jenn's possessions in one day. We managed to accomplish what was necessary, pray with the traumatized owner of the building where Jenn had died, and put together the memorial service for the next day. Her service was praiseworthy, I know, and although our family and friends mourned, it was not as those without hope. Jenn was a believer who had simply become overwhelmed by sickness and despair.

Exactly two weeks after her death, I was sitting at the breakfast room table around 5:30 on a Sunday morning having my quiet time with the Lord. Suddenly, without my even giving it a thought, the Holy Spirit gave me the meaning of the vision I had seen two weeks prior to Jenn's death: the billowy clouds did represent heaven; the red light was God's desire to stop her from taking her life; the green light was His permissive will in allowing her free choice. The scripture verse, "A house divided against itself cannot stand," spoke of the conflict Jenn had between knowing Jesus as her Savior and trying to live in the world with a sick mind and body. I believe that God was assuring us of her presence with Him in heaven, and it was the greatest gift I could have received. I felt the strength of His love—for her, for myself, and for our family.

Gary Oliver and his family endured the catastrophic loss of Matt on May 5, 2007, followed by Carrie's death less than two months later on July 2. Continuing the tradition of Carrie's journal, Gary has written monthly updates since that time which can be accessed on Carrie's website, www.carrieshealth.com. He wrote of the significance of commemorating Carrie's forty-ninth birthday without her.

Gary's Updates, May 1, 2008: There has been a lot of joy and laughter in April, but in many ways it was one of the most painful and difficult months since the death of Matt and Carrie. April 21st would have been Carrie's 49th birthday. Usually I would have been buying 4-5 cards, a couple silly, a couple serious, and one or two that only a husband should give to his wife and that nobody else should see. I would have purchased a couple of gifts and had a plan to try and surprise a woman who could never be surprised. Sometimes I thought Carrie knew what I was going to get her before I did. She was a real stinker that way. But, for the first time in 28 years, there was no one to buy cards and gifts for and I found myself missing her and missing doing those little things in ways I hadn't anticipated. The week of April 21st was a rough week with a number of emotional "ambushes" and her birthday was a day of both sorrow and celebration, but while I had a lot of tears, it was in all honesty mostly about celebration. At times it's still very hard to believe that she is no longer here and at the same time there is a ton of good things to remember and a lot to be thankful for—and I choose joy.

Someone once wrote that grief is like walking through molasses. So true. I'm also learning that grief is like a smoke alarm. It can be triggered by bacon burning or by your house burning. It doesn't matter how much smoke there is or how big the fire; once the alarm is triggered, the volume of the alarm is the same. Maybe I'm becoming aware of the cumulative impact of the many physical, emotional, financial and relational losses over the last four years. The phenomenal alone-ness. The loss of plans and dreams that will never be realized.

I think I've become more aware than ever of our human frailty and how fragile the heart can be. In the midst of the losses, there is always the reality of the fact that: "Because of the Lord's great love we are not consumed, for his compassions never fail. They are new every morning; great is your faithfulness. I say to myself, 'The Lord is my portion; therefore I will wait for Him'" (Lamentations 3:22-24) and then, "Though He brings grief, He will show compassion, so great is his unfailing love" (Lamentations 3:32).[49]

Nearly two years earlier, Carrie wrote of another commemoration: the first anniversary of her cancer diagnosis. Although their words and styles of expression are dissimilar, the common link is the love of God that supersedes all circumstances, even disease and death, and that surpasses all knowledge.

CARRIE

Journal entry, May 15, 2006: So what does this anniversary feel like as I walk through it this week? I celebrate this year anniversary, not necessarily the diagnosis, but I celebrate a year of life, perhaps more living than I have ever lived. I celebrate relationships, my family, my friends and those that I pray for and that uphold me in prayer. I celebrate scripture and truth and healing and holiness. I celebrate finding Jesus to be all that he says He is, and trusting Him to strengthen me in my loneliest of moments and to believe that His love is really all I ever need, even while living on this earth. I celebrate the working out of His purpose, in His kingdom, through this cancer experience. I am in awe of what He has done and am deeply humbled. This anniversary is a "marker" of God's tremendous love.

In the scope of eternity, these words spoken out of chronological order make sense. God's truth prevails, because God is Truth. His mercies endure forever. His love is from everlasting to everlasting. He will never leave us or forsake us. Jesus Christ is the same yesterday, today and forever. He died that we might live. God is love. This we can celebrate through all eternity!

Heavenly Father, without you, we can do nothing; with you, all things are possible. You are the Lord of the brokenhearted, and the God of all hope. We look to you as we commemorate these anniversaries of loss, knowing that in you we find Life. In Jesus' name, Amen.

Consequently, you are no longer foreigners and aliens, but fellow citizens with God's people and members of God's household, built on the foundation of the apostles and prophets, with Christ Jesus himself as the chief cornerstone. In Him the whole building is joined together and rises to become a holy temple in the Lord. And in Him you too are being built together to become a dwelling in which God lives by His Spirit. —Ephesians 2:19-22

36

Glimpses

CARRIE

*Journal entry, April 17, 2007: I began to look at my own life in terms of "a glimpse." Is God giving me a glimpse of some sort? What is real that I can live right now, and what is it He has for me in heaven with Him? How much heaven can we really have on earth? Wow! What a question. I know God has been showing me heaven with Him. I do believe that much of what He is showing me is something we can already have with Him, but for so many of us we are too involved in other things in our lives to catch this glimpse, let alone live the glimpse of living "heaven on earth." In my glimpse, I have been driven to go to God. I cannot exist without Him. This past week was another example of this as I arrived home from M.D. Anderson on April 10th. Coming home, the rain and the cold felt awful. Coming home felt sad and lonely. The fluid on my stomach seemed overwhelming. I felt closed in. This was not a penthouse dream. It was more of an earthly yucky feeling and perspective. In spite of my feelings, I did keep going, keeping commitments, attending dinners with the JBU board of trustees, talking about the book (*Grown-Up Girlfriends*) with some ladies with Erin (Smalley), presenting with Gary, going out on Saturday with Erin to spend the day as our husbands were gone. By Sunday morning, though, my heart felt low and lonely and I could not* *get the "glimpse of heaven" that I know in my heart that God wants me to experience. I called three prayer warriors that are close to me. Each prayer warrior had something precious to give. Each prayer warrior gave me a glimpse of who God is in the midst of my experience, and on Sunday, I began to live the glimpse of heaven again right here on this earth. I was reminded of the fact that there is no fear in God's perfect love, that God does have a future and plan for me and a hope. God loves healing His children. Loves it! That at the last moment when Abraham was about to sacrifice his son, God stopped him and said, "I see you are obedient." Abraham saw the ram in the thicket that would be the sacrifice, not his beloved son. Jesus, of course, is our Ram. He died in place for us. One prayer warrior reminded me that Eve knew no fear before the fall. She only knew of God's perfect love for her. Oh, the glimpse of feeling, experiencing the perfect love of God without any fear whatsoever!*

Some of you are like me. You have been thrown into the opportunity to catch a glimpse, but you know that Satan would convince us that unless we walk tragedy, heaven is not something we can experience and if it takes trauma, then maybe we don't want it! My nightmare really has turned into a dream. Even when it is hard, I would rather live this closeness to Jesus; this closeness to heaven.

Although we are pilgrims passing through this earth on the way to our heavenly home, we have been taught by Jesus to pray:

> Our Father who art in heaven, hallowed be thy name; thy kingdom come, thy will be done on earth as it is in heaven. Give us today our daily bread, and forgive us our debts, as we forgive our debtors. And lead us not into temptation, but deliver us from evil" (Matthew 6:9-13).

Later manuscripts add, "For thine is the Kingdom, and the power, and the glory forever," and this is how we commonly pray. If Jesus has told us that His Father's will is to be done on earth as it is in heaven, and that God's Kingdom, power and glory are forever, then heaven is on earth right now and accessible to all who humble themselves and call Jesus their Savior and Lord!

How do we live heaven on earth? The Old Testament patriarch Jacob had a taste of it that we read about in Genesis 28:12-17:

> He had a dream in which he saw a stairway resting on the earth, with its top reaching to heaven, and the angels of God were ascending and descending on it. There above it stood the Lord, and He said, "I am the Lord, the God of your father Abraham and the God of Isaac. I will give you and your descendants the land on which you are lying. Your descendants will be like the dust of the earth, and you will spread out to the west and to the east, to the north and to the south. All peoples on earth will be blessed through you and your offspring. I am with you and will watch over you wherever you go, and I will bring you back to this land. I will not leave you until I have done what I have promised you." When Jacob awoke from his sleep, he thought, "Surely the Lord is in this place, and I was not aware of it." He was afraid and said, "How awesome is this place! This is none other than the house of God; this is the gate of heaven."

How often are we aware that the Lord is in this place called earth? We are so frenetically pursuing what we think life is all about that we miss the Reason we have life! Do we "hallow" God's name, or do we parrot a phrase that is as banal as "no problem"? Are we grateful for our daily bread, or do we whine because it isn't always steak? What kind of shape would we be in if God forgave us in the grudging way we sometimes forgive others? Do we really desire to be protected from temptation, or do we want to insert a selective clause? When He provides a way out of evil, do we even choose to take it? These questions are all deeply convicting to me, as I have been guilty of every one of them. It is only by the grace of God through the gift of Jesus Christ that my life has been changed, and that I am determined to see His Kingdom come on earth as it is in heaven.

My journey through cancer, the loss of my babies, the subsequent multiple surgeries, my accidents, the deaths of my father and sister—and I know it's not over yet—have all pointed me towards pursuing His Kingdom here on earth. I have a hunger for God that is insatiable, because He is the Bread of life and the only true sustenance, and I feast on His Word. I have a thirst for Him that will never be quenched in this life, but I drink from the Living Water that is Christ. I have struggled to have my own way time after time, only to discover that HE is the Way. The 17th-century French philosopher, theologian and mathematician Blaise Pascal said, "There is a God-shaped vacuum in the heart of every man which cannot be filled by any created thing, but only by God, the Creator, made known through Jesus." It is only the presence of the risen Savior that can fill us and make us whole, that can bring His Kingdom on earth as it is in heaven.

We need to learn to live with the mind of Christ: that transformed and renewed way of thinking that views things from an eternal perspective. So often there are occurrences in daily life that seem to be coincidental, but are really so much evidence of God's presence and desire to bring heaven to earth. The intimacy and intricacy of His plan is something that can only be attributed to divine design!

How could one possibly explain in human terms the way in which I met Carrie Oliver in January of 2006? Although we had both lived in the Denver area for several years and had close mutual friends, it was not until our pastor, Stew Grant, asked me to come alongside her as she underwent treatment at M.D. Anderson that we actually met. This was only because Stew was working on his doctorate and Gary Oliver was the director of his project, despite the fact that Stew lived in Texas, Gary resided in Arkansas, and the seminary was in Colorado. It was only because Philippe and I had been active in the prayer, healing and caring ministry that we really knew Stew, and it was only because I had been a cancer patient myself that I was drawn to this ministry.

God knew all along! He desired for heaven and earth to come together in this relationship that would bear much fruit for His Kingdom!

God did not "give" either Carrie or me cancer; it happened because we live in a world where there is sickness, suffering and evil. But we were both absolutely aware of the knowledge that He has overcome the world. We have hungered and thirsted after Him for righteousness' sake, and ours has become the Kingdom of heaven: mine still on earth, and Carrie's in heaven.

God has given me glimpses of heaven on earth in ways that He speaks of in Acts 2:17-18, "In the last days, God says, I will pour out my Spirit on all people. Your sons and daughters will prophesy, your young men will see visions, your old men will dream dreams."

On July 14, 2000, the Lord knew I was still grieving over the loss of our children before birth in 1990. Around 11:30 that night, I was in a sort of "twilight" slumber and suddenly saw the image of a beautiful little girl with long blonde curls wearing a flowing white dress come running to me in my bed. I was shocked by the authenticity of the vision, and immediately asked the Lord to interpret it for me.

"Who is she, Lord?" By the power of the Holy Spirit, he told me that this was our daughter that I had lost during the surgery ten years previously, and that her name was HOPE. I said, "But Lord, you know I wouldn't have named my daughter 'Hope'!" The Holy Spirit then guided me in my spirit to Romans 5 where Paul talks about suffering:

> And we rejoice in the HOPE of the glory of God. Not only so, but we also rejoice in our sufferings, because we know that suffering produces perseverance; perseverance, character; and character, HOPE. And HOPE does not disappoint us, because God has poured out His love into our hearts by the Holy Spirit, whom He has given us.

God had allowed His Kingdom to come on earth to give me

HOPE. And I have HOPE in heaven—both my HOPE and His HOPE!

A poignant memory just surfaced from the tumultuous days following my diagnosis of endometrial cancer in May of 1990. My beloved mother came to stay with Philippe and me as we sought God's plan for my healing. Attending the Saturday Sabbath service together at Cherry Creek Presbyterian church, we stood to sing the final hymn, Fanny Crosby's "Blessed Assurance." With wavering voice and blinding tears, I struggled to affirm the truth of these potent words:

> Blessed assurance, Jesus is mine!
> O what a foretaste of glory divine!
> Heir of salvation, purchase of God,
> born of His Spirit, washed in His blood.
> This is my story, this is my song,
> praising my Savior all the day long;
> This is my story, this is my song,
> praising my Savior all the day long.
>
> Perfect submission, perfect delight!
> Visions of rapture now burst on my sight;
> Angels descending bring from above
> echoes of mercy, whispers of love.
> This is my story, this is my song,
> praising my Savior all the day long;
> This is my story, this is my song,
> praising my Savior all the day long.
>
> Perfect submission—all is at rest,
> I in my Savior am happy and blest;
> Watching and waiting, looking above,
> filled with His goodness, lost in His love.
> This is my story, this is my song,
> praising my Savior all the day long.

This is my story, this is my song,
praising my Savior all the day long.

Bolstered and girded by the faith of my family and friends surrounding me, I sensed in my viscera the absolute truth of Hebrews
11:1: "Now faith is being sure of what we hope for and certain of
what we do not see." I could not see further than the hymnal in
front of my own face, but I had an ineffable and blessed assurance
that Jesus is mine. Now this is my story and this is my song.

"You also must be ready, for the Son of Man will come at an
hour when you do not expect Him" (Luke 12:40). I thought that
day had arrived a few years ago when, at the stroke of midnight,
I was awakened from a deep sleep by the blast of a trumpet! I sat
bolt upright in bed and shouted, "Jesus has come back!" Imagine my
utter dismay when I realized that a power outage had reset the timer
on our home intercom and sound system, and I was only hearing
the climax of a Bruckner or Mahler symphony! But we don't know
when that hour will be that God calls us home forever. We must
keep the oil in our lamps burning and our hearts on fire for Him!

CARRIE

*Journal entry, April 17, 2007: Won't you live the glimpse with me?! Live
heaven on earth! If you don't know what that means, then go looking for it. Pray
the Lord's Prayer: "Your will be done on earth as it is in heaven." Amen.*

> **Almighty and eternal God**, King of kings and Lord
> of lords, what great rejoicing there will be when we are
> all together in your presence forever! Help us to live
> your Kingdom now on earth as it will be in heaven.
> Let us show others the way to your Kingdom that they
> may also have life everlasting. We pray in the name of
> Jesus, whose love endures forever, Amen and Amen!

Afterword

Cancer! The dreaded diagnosis means transition. How you view yourself, your marriage, your children, your important relationships, your priorities, your values, and your future will never be the same. In fact, it may even impact your view of God: His goodness, His mercy, His character and His promises. It will also impact how others see you and treat you.

I remember making a home visit to a woman in one of my churches who was fighting for her life in her battle against cancer. She and her husband had been leaders in the church for many years. He was an elder; she had started the women's ministry, had a flourishing discipleship ministry and had impacted thousands of women. She was lying on the couch and was clearly weak. Sometime during our conversation, she said the biggest surprise since her diagnosis was that many people stopped calling her and few came to visit her. "Gary," she said, "it's like I have leprosy. People don't know what to say or how to deal with people like me."

It will force you to redefine normal. In fact, you will have to find a "new" normal. But not only does it force you to redefine aspects of your life, I've discovered that it can also provide an opportunity to become refined as gold purified by fire. You are forced with a choice: you can be a victim who is defined by the diagnosis, or you can learn what it means to become "more than a conqueror." During my adventures with cancer over the past 25 years of my life, I've been given eyes that see things I'd never noticed before; ears that hear with a new acuity and clarity; a heart that is much more sensitive. I've grown spiritually, emotionally and relationally.

Spiritually

In the spiritual dimension, dealing with cancer in my own life and in the life of my late wife Carrie has given me the opportunity to better understand the power of perspective. Most people go through life with a problem-focus. Their cup is always half-empty and they are experts on what could be better, on what others have that they don't have, on who is better off than they are and how they would be happier if their circumstances were different.

Cancer has helped me develop more of a promise-focus. That simply means that the reality of the day-in and day-out struggle in dealing with cancer in my own life and in the lives of those I love has given me the opportunity to see the promises in God's word from a whole new perspective. When I look at my life in light of what God has promised, it becomes much easier to move from a fear-focus to a faith-focus.

I remember when I was at a Promise Keepers board meeting many years ago and I had just been given my third diagnosis of cancer and was scheduled for surgery the next week. Coach Bill McCartney had the board members come around me and lay hands on me as they prayed. After the prayer, Dr. Howard Hendricks, who was sitting next to me and who had just come through a long surgery for skin cancer, turned to me, put his hand on my knee, looked me in the eyes and said, "Gary, when they were taking me into surgery, I sensed God saying to me, 'Hendricks, your whole life you've told people that I'm sovereign. Well, either I am or I'm not.'" I never forgot those words. In fact, in every subsequent surgery as I've gone under the anesthetic, I've thanked God that He is sovereign and that I can trust Him. It does make a difference.

As dealing with the diagnosis forced me into God's word, I felt led to study the word "joy" and came up with some amazing discoveries. Did you know that a primary objective in Jesus' teaching was that His disciples might experience JOY? Did you know that the words joy/joyous/joyful are found over 200 times in scripture? Did you know that the verb rejoice appears well over 200 times as well?

Look at these verses:

- In thy presence is fullness of JOY; in thy right hand there are pleasures forever (Psalm 16:11).

- For His anger is but for a moment, His favor is for a lifetime. Weeping may last for the night, but a shout of JOY comes in the morning (Psalm 30:5).

- I take JOY in doing your will, my God, for your law is written on my heart (Psalm 40:8).

- These things I have spoken to you so that you may be filled with my JOY and that your JOY may overflow (John 15:11).

- Truly, truly I say to you, that you will weep and lament...but your sorrow will be turned to JOY. If you shall ask the Father for anything, He will give it to you in My name. Until now you have asked nothing in My name; ask, and you will receive, that your JOY may be made full (John 16:20, 23-24).

EMOTIONALLY

In addition to spiritual growth, I've also had the opportunity to experience significant emotional growth. I grew up in Long Beach, California, and on the beach there was an amusement park called The Pike. The Pike was home to the world's largest (at that time) wooden roller coaster. The ride was called the Cyclone Racer, and when I was in middle school, it only cost 50 cents a ride. I still remember the day I had saved my money and went on it 10 times in a row.

A roller coaster is fun to ride but wouldn't be much fun to live on. Dealing with the diagnosis of cancer can put you and those you love on the emotional roller coaster ride of your lives. It provides a greater opportunity to learn when you can trust your emotions and when you can't. Fear, discouragement, depression, anger and anxiety are just a few of the emotions you will face. In dealing with cancer, I had to face these emotions head-on and decide if I was going to believe some of their lies and let them determine my reality, or take them captive to what I knew to be true. I remember many days that I would have to remind myself that "feelings don't always equal facts," and when success looked a lot like simply putting one foot in front of the other.

RELATIONALLY

One of the main gifts of dealing with cancer has been to learn in a new way and at a whole new level the healing power of friends. Some of my friends have "taken me to school" on how to provide love and support at a time when you have no idea what you need and are just hoping to be able to make it through the day.

I've learned in a whole new way the power of presence—just being there sometimes without anything to say except "I don't know what to say but I love you and am here with you;" the power of a voicemail, e-mail or text message with no expectation of a response; the repeated reassurance that I was being prayed for; a verse or a poem. I was amazed by the number of notes I received from people that I've never met. Any expression of concern or of prayer is encouraging, but to receive one and two-page handwritten notes from total strangers was astonishing and a profound source of encouragement.

SO NOW WHAT?

It's all about choices. As Howard Hendricks told me, either God is sovereign or He isn't. Either we can trust Him or we can't. Either

He is just a promise-maker or He is also a promise-KEEPER, and so much of it is a matter of perspective. As Oswald Chambers wrote:

> The circumstances of a saint's life are ordained of God. In the life of a saint there is no such thing as chance. God by His providence brings you into circumstances that you can't understand at all, but the Spirit of God understands. God brings you to places, among people, and into certain conditions to accomplish a definite purpose through the intercession of the Spirit in you...all your circumstances are in the hand of God, and therefore you don't ever have to think they are unnatural or unique (*My Utmost for His Highest*, November 7).

On a very personal note please know that this isn't just a bunch of theory for me. Since I first committed to write this there have been even more significant changes in my life. After two years of being single God brought a delightful woman into my life and, after 15 months of dating and engagement on April 3, 2010 (the Saturday before Easter Sunday), we were married. Linda is a remarkable woman who loves the Lord, family and friends, and God has given us a great love for each other. With her two adult children and my two adult children we both have the increased joy of expanded families.

One month after our wedding I received my sixth diagnosis of cancer. I underwent a 10-hour surgery with a long recuperation, the first month of which was in bed. In addition to being my wife and my friend, Linda is also a skilled and compassionate nurse with many years of experience providing care in intensive care units, so she was well prepared to care for me during my recovery. But that wasn't the final, nor the greatest, challenge.

In November of that same year, as I was making good progress and steadily improving, I received my seventh diagnosis of cancer. This time I was told it was inoperable. As I write this, I have just finished more chemotherapy treatments with all of the lousy side effects that come with it. I thought my chemo regimen in 2003 was nasty, but this time I felt like I'd been hit by a Mack truck.

Throughout all of this God has been very present to me in the form of my precious wife Linda, my extended family, and many dear friends. In a very real world facing very real problems we have been able to experience God's power and presence and the sovereign joy that can only come from a personal relationship with Him.

I've learned that success in life is not primarily how long I live but how well I live, with whatever time I have left. I don't like cancer. Every nasty thing anyone has ever said about cancer is true. At the same time, God can use cancer to help you surrender the illusion of control.

In some ways I wish this wasn't the case. But after having spent hundreds of hours hiking, fishing and backpacking in the Sierras, Tetons and Rockies, I can say that while I love the mountaintops, the honest truth is that my greatest life lessons, and perhaps the things that have allowed me to have the greatest impact on others, have come out of what I've learned from my time spent in the dark and difficult valleys.

Cancer can be a great reminder that time is precious. Relationships are precious. Every day I have, I can choose to focus on the problems or on the promises. I can choose a fear-focus or a faith-focus. I can choose to be the puppet of my problems and a slave to my circumstances. I can choose to be more than conquered by the cancer, or in the words of Romans 8, I can choose to be more than a conqueror. And that's a choice I make every single day.

For several months, I've been keeping a list of things that cancer can and can't do. It's still growing but here is my list so far:

CANCER CAN:

    Be very painful
    Lead to very painful emotions

End my life earlier than I'd anticipated
Add new limitations to what I can do
Get me to focus on what I've lost and what I can't do
Distort my perspective...if I let it
Increase my sense of hopelessness
Make me aware of my "inattentional blindness"
Help me place a new value on relationships
Force me to focus
Make me slow down and be still (which energizer bunnies find difficult)
Make me realize the "end" may be closer than I thought
Allow me to prepare accordingly
Remind me to do things I haven't done
Help me notice things I haven't noticed before
Give friends a unique opportunity to be "real" friends
Help me see some new blessings I wasn't aware of
Teach me new things to be thankful for
Introduce me to new friends
Give me new eyes to see the hurts and needs of others
Increase my appreciation for things I've taken for granted
Help me become a better listener to God and others

CANCER CAN'T:

Rob me of my joy
Keep me from learning
Keep me from loving
Keep me from being loved
Keep me from growing
Keep me from encouraging others
Keep me from laughing
Keep me from claiming God's promises
Keep me from praising God for what I still can do
Rob me of my friends

Shatter my hope
Destroy my faith
Suppress the many precious memories I have
Defeat the power of God's Spirit that lives within me
Take away my eternal life

Cancer has taught me the power of God's promises, the value of healthy emotions, and the significance of healthy relationships. God has given me the strength to respond in ways that have caused it to become an opportunity to see God, myself, my family, my friends, my vocation and my life in new ways. I'm not thankful for the cancer, but I'm enormously grateful for God's goodness, grace, mercy, faithfulness and loving-kindness in the midst of the battle.

Blessed be the God and Father of our Lord Jesus Christ, the Father of mercies and God of all comfort, who comforts us in all of our affliction so that we will be able to comfort those who are in any affliction with the comfort with which we ourselves are comforted by God. For just as the sufferings of Christ are ours in abundance, so also our comfort is abundant through Christ. But if we are afflicted, it is for your comfort and salvation, or if we are comforted, it is for your comfort, which is effective in the patient enduring of the same sufferings which we also suffer, and our hope for you is firmly grounded, knowing that as you are sharers of our sufferings, so also you are sharers of our comfort. For we do not want you to be unaware, brethren, of our affliction which came to us in Asia, that we were burdened excessively, beyond our strength, so that we despaired even of life; indeed, we had the sentence of death within ourselves so that we would not trust in ourselves, but in God who raises the dead, who delivered us from so great a peril of death, and will deliver us, He on whom we have set our hope (II Corinthians 1:3-10, NASB).

Gary J. Oliver, Th.M., Ph.D.

Notes

1. R.Norman Herbert, *Hymns and Poems – God Among His People* (Unpublished work, 1979). Used by permission.

2. Oswald Chambers, *My Utmost for His Highest* (New York: Dodd, Mead and Company, 1967), 335.

3. Marilynne E. Foster, *Tozer on the Holy Spirit* (Camp Hill, PA: Christian Publications, Inc., 2000), June 16 excerpt.

4. Eugene Peterson, *The Message Remix* (Colorado Springs, Co: Alive Communications, 2003).

5. Henri Nouwen, *The Life of the Beloved* (New York.: Crossroad Publishing Co., 1992).

6. Richard J. Foster and James Bryan Smith, editors, *Devotional Classics* (San Francisco: Harper/Renovare, 1990), 243.

7. Bob Sorge, *Secrets of the Secret Place* (Greenwood, MO: Oasis House, 2001), 124.

8. Bill Johnson, *The Supernatural Power of a Transformed Mind* (Shippensburg, PA: Destiny Image Publishers, Inc., 2005), 123-124.

9. Erin Smalley and Carrie Oliver, *Grown-Up Girlfriends* (Carol Stream, IL: Tyndale House Publishers, 2007), 33.

10. Ibid., 176-177.

11. Ibid., 179-180.

12. Donna Fargo, *A Girlfriend is a Sister You Choose* (Blue Mountain Arts, 2005).

13. Erin Smalley and Carrie Oliver, *Grown-Up Girlfriends* (Carol Stream, IL: Tyndale House Publishers, 2007), 23.

14. John Bunyon, *The Pilgrim's Progress* (Orleans, MA: Paraclete Press, 1982), preface.

15. Oswald Chambers, *My Utmost for His Highest* (New York: Dodd, Mead and

Company, 1967), 214.

16. Bob Sorge, *Secrets of the Secret Place* (Greenwood, MO: Oasis House, 2001), 191-192.

17. Oswald Chambers, *My Utmost for His Highest* (New York: Dodd, Mead and Company,1967), 115.

18. Erin Smalley and Carrie Oliver, *Grown-Up Girlfriends* (Carol Stream, IL: Tyndale House Publishers, 2007), 200, 205.

19. Gary J. Oliver and Carrie Oliver, *Mad About Us* (Bloomington, MN: Bethany House Publishers, 2007), 171.

20. Ibid., 172.

21. Elisabeth Kübler-Ross, *On Death and Dying* (New York: Touchstone, 1997).

22. Gary and Carrie Oliver, *Raising Sons and Loving It* (Grand Rapids, MI: Zondervan, 2000), 136-137.

23. C.S. Lewis, *A Grief Observed* (New York: Bantam Books, 1961), 1-2.

24. Richard J. Foster and James Bryan Smith, ed., *Devotional Classics* (San Francisco: Harper/Renovare, 1990), 166-167.

25. Henry T. Blackaby and Richard Blackaby, *Experiencing God Day-by-Day* (Nashville, TN: Broadman and Holman Publishers, 1997), 48-49.

26. Oswald Chambers, *My Utmost for His Highest* (New York: Dodd, Mead and Company,1967), 223.

27. Ibid., 306.

28. Marilynne E. Foster, *Tozer on the Holy Spirit* (Camp Hill, PA: Christian Publications, Inc., 2000), July 21 excerpt.

29. Oswald Chambers, *My Utmost for His Highest* (New York: Dodd, Mead and Company,1967), 215.

30. Ibid., 215.

31. Chris Rice, "Untitled Hymn: Come to Jesus" from *Run the Earth Watch the Sky* (Rocketown Records 2003).

32. Marilynne E. Foster, *Tozer on the Holy Spirit* (Camp Hill, PA: Christian Publications, Inc., 2000), July 9 excerpt.

33. Bob Sorge, *Secrets of the Secret Place* (Greenwood, MO: Oasis House, 2001), 167-168.

34. Brennan Manning, *The Importance of Being Foolish: How to Think Like Jesus* (New York: HarperCollins, 2005), 175.

35. Ibid., 5.

36. Ibid., 38.

37. Ibid., 47.

38. Kefa Sempangi, *A Distant Grief* (Glendale, CA: Regal Books Division, G/L Publications,1979), 119.

39. Ibid., 119-120.

40. Gary Oliver, "Sovereign Joy" message: www.liferelationships.com. Used by permission.

41. Oswald Chambers, *My Utmost for His Highest* (New York: Dodd, Mead and Company, 1967), 244.

42. Bob Sorge, *Secrets of the Secret Place* (Greenwood, MO: Oasis House, 2001), 122.

43. Gary J. Oliver, journal update, www.carrieshealth.com, May 1, 2008. Used by permission.

44. Hannah Hurnard, *Walking Among the Unseen* (Carol Stream, IL: Tyndale House Publishers, 1977), 99.

45. Jonathan Edwards, "Religious Affections," in *Devotional Classics*, eds. Richard J. Foster and James Bryan Smith (San Francisco: Harper/Renovare, 1990), 20-21.

46. Ibid., 22.

47. John Donne, "Meditation XVII," *Devotions Upon Emergent Occasions,* 1624.

48. Hannah Hurnard, *Walking Among the Unseen* (Carol Stream, IL: Tyndale House Publishers, 1977), 139-140.

49. Gary J. Oliver, journal update, May 1, 2008. Used by permission.

Jan de Chambrier

is first and foremost a servant and friend of the Lord Jesus Christ.
A professional musician and faculty member of the Shepherd
School of Music at Rice University for fifteen years, her primary
calling is to minister to others with the light and love of Christ.
Jan serves in lay ministry along with her husband, Philippe, at The
Woodlands United Methodist Church in The Woodlands, TX,
where they have helped to build the prayer and healing ministry.
The de Chambrier family, including their son Paul, is active in mis-
sions and established the Uganda Book Project after visiting one
of their sponsored children through Compassion International in
2007. Jan and Philippe are affiliated with International Leadership
Institute and have taught at conferences in Brazil, Czech Republic,
Colombia, Belize and Ukraine. One of Jan's great joys is to mentor young adults, including former Rice University students as well
as those she has met at ILI History Maker conferences. She also
serves as a peer mentor to newly-diagnosed cancer patients at the
M.D. Anderson Cancer Center. Born in Chicago and the daughter
of a Presbyterian minister, she has had a lifelong love of music. Jan
earned two degrees in piano from Northwestern University and
has had extensive experience as a performing artist, including many
television and radio broadcasts, and has also been a radio announcer
on classical radio station KVOD in Denver, Colorado.

Carrie Oliver

dedicated her life to loving and serving Jesus Christ, and went home to be with Him forever on July 2, 2007. Carrie was the wife of her beloved Gary Oliver, and together they raised three sons, Nathan, Matt and Andrew. She served in ministry with Gary as a clinical counselor and marriage and family conference speaker, both nationally and internationally, and was also on the faculty of John Brown University. Carrie co-authored over 100 magazine articles and three other books, *Raising Sons and Loving It!* and *Mad about Us* (with Dr. Gary Oliver), and *Grown-Up Girlfriends* (with Erin Smalley). Born to Marilyn and Vic Webster on April 21, 1959, Carrie was raised in central Nebraska and later earned degrees with high honors from the University of Nebraska and Denver Seminary, and was committed to helping others find the fullness of life in Christ. Following her diagnosis of pancreatic cancer in May of 2005, Carrie ministered to countless individuals through "A Journal of Hope" on her website, www.carrieshealth.com, which is still active. It was this online journal that formed the basis for Carrie's voice in this book. Carrie Oliver and Jan de Chambrier were sisters of the heart.